Pra

"There are many books on how t   . This is the first to show what it will take to build ＿＿＿＿＿＿＿＿＿＿＿＿＿＿＿tury."

"I loved "Brand Shift"! It provides an insightful look into the future of how brands will be marketed. Houle and Shapiro address the trends and challenges marketing professionals will face in the future and offer clear concepts and strategies to ensure that CMOs can succeed in the years ahead. I finally have a clearer view of where to go!"

"By offering a thorough understanding of the history of brands and how technology, artificial intelligence, and Big Data will influence marketing trends, Houle and Shapiro deliver a compelling strategy for navigating the inevitable global shifts already challenging marketing professionals."

"I've known David Houle since he was part of our team at MTV as we re-invented how brands connected to consumers in that era. Today, as media continues to evolve and brands are seeking to effectively connect with consumers wherever they are, on multiple platforms and devices, Houle and his co-author Shapiro are helping marketers understand how to make those connections now."

"Successful marketers embrace change as an opportunity to build stronger brands. "Brand Shift" provides a fascinating look at future social and technological changes that will create disruptive and powerful brand marketing opportunities. A must read for those responsible for future brand marketing."

"*Brand Shift* is for anyone and everyone who has anything to do with surviving and thriving is today's turbulent, mobile, digital, instantaneous, real time, 'Big Data' brand environment."

"In a time when some argue that brands matter less, I'm the firmest believer that people need to connect with strong brands more than ever. This is a fascinating portrayal of how social and technological changes in the Shift Age will transform the future of brand marketing."

Tom Trenta - Chief Strategist, Egg Strategy

"The future of brands and branding is here - IF you read this book. Houle and Shapiro's ability to articulate future trends is invaluable to anyone that is in the business of managing a brand. Brand storytelling is going through significant changes and the Brand Shift is the roadmap. Read it. Now."

Dave Kustin - Founder, Content Bacon

"David Houle could probably pick all the winners at the race track. I'd like to take him to Las Vegas but meantime I'll read "Brand Shift", written with Owen Shapiro, to find out how to take advantage of the next hot trends in marketing."

Bob Sirott - WGN Chicago Broadcast Personality

"Bravo! This book is not only essential for all levels of marketing employees and students, it's a 'must' read for all business professionals. The future, which is now defined as tomorrow, requires significant changes in marketing/branding to remain competitive. This insightful guide to the future is an excellent tool, so well written and organized that the concepts are easily grasped."

Richard J. Kaplan
VP Marketing,
RCAD
Former President, Chief Brand Officer
Tervis Tumbler Co.

"It's easy to be aware that branding is changing, but exceptionally difficult to know where it's going. This book clearly demonstrates that Owen and David's understanding of the future of branding is unmatched in their industry."

Seth Kravitz - CEO of Technori / Former CEO of InsuranceAgents.com

"A fascinating and thought provoking portrayal of how social and technological changes in the Shift Age will transform the future of brand marketing."

Sam Guren (30+ years as professional principle investor in venture capital/private equity)

BRAND SHIFT

THE FUTURE OF BRANDS AND MARKETING

DAVID HOULE + OWEN SHAPIRO

David Houle & Associates

To Victoria, with love and gratitude.

David

To Lum, Julius, Richard, and Rockwell,
you are my beginning, end, and everything in-between

Owen

at a time when animals were frequently sacrificed. There, in the shadow of Mount Sapo, rain washed tallow (rendered beef fat) from sacrificial cattle down the mountain, mixing it with ashes, and then depositing it in the clay that lay along the Tiber River. The clay mixture, it turned out, made dishwashing easier than ever. With that, soap was born.

Soap improved over time, but consistently remained a product that was crudely manufactured in small batches and sold locally. That is, until the advent of the Industrial Age. That's when bar soaps were produced with much higher quality and lower costs (and in less time), driving out the local producers. Bars of soap were literally branded with the product's own name, and Ivory became P&G's first product—and one of the very earliest advertised products—to use the product sample, itself, as a marketing tool. Look around the soap section at your local drug store today. You will see that manufacturing processes—and branding—haven't changed. While locally made, small-batch artisanal soap is still available in specialty shops, Ivory, Dove, Dial, Olay and other mass-produced brands are less expensive and much more widely available.

In the 20th century, we also saw the rise of the national brand. As large companies continued replacing mom-and-pop producers, brands became a vehicle for actually bringing together a vast number of disparate communities into a single market, uniting an entire country. Not surprisingly, the early brands often picked up on patriotic American themes that reinforced the common culture and tastes of the U.S. market. Uncle Sam is a prime example.

While Uncle Sam evolved over the years, the illustration of the Uncle Sam that we recognize today grew from Thomas Nates' depictions of the character, including those in the 1860s. Uncle Sam symbolized not only the U.S. government, but in some cases, society as a whole. He emerged following the Civil War, when feelings of patriotism and pride over the federal (i.e., national) government were running extremely high. Uncle Sam became an icon for the American people.

In the book *How Brands Become Icons: The Principles of Cultural Branding*, author Douglas B. Holt analyzes the ways that certain brands manage to transcend the product they represent and become philosophies and cultural representations, in and of themselves. Holt says brands can surpass the idea of a "trademark" and reach a deeper level when they help people mediate an unresolved emotional crisis (a.k.a. core dissonance). The most successful early American brands did just that by bringing together a country made up of isolated communities, relatively disconnected immigrant populations, and a common vernacular and brand habits. It was around these brands that men, women, and children of all ages and backgrounds could develop a shared interest and taste.

By the 1920s and 1930s, brands changed focus from American patriotism to urbanism, as the country became more centralized around cities. Brands that captured this spirit often embraced art deco graphics and images, which communicated a modern, sophisticated air. Just as patriotic branding had helped unify the country, so too did urbanism, which allowed rural dwellers and recent immigrants access to the same modern and cutting-edge products that were designed for the tastes and lifestyles of the movers and shakers in America's larger cities. It was in this period—1922, to be exact—that radio advertising began, bringing brands into people's homes and heads while also monetizing the medium for the first time.

The use of patriotic branding is an example of brands addressing what Maslow defines as the Social Needs, by helping consumers feel connected and accepted during a period when ethnic groups and geographic groups are knitting themselves into a single American culture.

The Second Golden Age of Brands

Then came television. Shortly after World War II, TV began transfixing more and more households. Shows like "The Ed Sullivan Show," "Meet the Press," and "The Jackie Gleason Show" became a part of the American vernacular, as programs became a shared cultural experience. According to the Federal Communications

Commission (FCC), sales of televisions increased by 500 percent between 1945 and 1948. By 1960, 85 percent of U.S. households had a TV. With that kind of meteoric rise, it comes as little surprise that television became the greatest technology for brand development of the 20th century.

Given the authors' familiarity with brands, it is hard to discuss them without bringing in some of their own personal experiences. Growing up in the 1950s and 1960s, they are classified as official baby boomers, raised on the "golden age" of brands, or the period between the end of World War II (circa 1950) and the dismantling of the network television oligopoly (1980s). During this period, major consumer brands played a giant game of chess, building and positioning themselves through massive advantages in marketing dollars, with relatively little ability for consumers to resist their messages (three television channels, few remotes, no commercial zapping). Those growing up during this period can remember watching astronauts mixing Tang, listening to the popping sounds of the Kellogg's Rice Krispies jingle in the 1960s and 1970s, and—discovering the Sony Walkman through TV ads.

The key levers in this game of strategy were typically:

- Pride in America
- Television advertising
- Production capacity to supply significant/dominant market share

One of the key examples of success in this approach is General Motors' Chevrolet division, which was at the forefront of the infusion of television into the evolution of brands. GM used innovative techniques in television to maintain a 25 percent market share for Chevrolet in the U.S. car market throughout the 1950s and 1960s.

According to *Advertising Age*, Chevrolet kicked off the decade of the 1950s with "the greatest outlay for advertising in the history of the automotive industry." They went on to note, "an innovation in the campaign will be widespread use of television." The theme of the campaign tightly intertwined patriotism, the American landscape, and Chevrolet, using the theme, "America's best seller, America's best buy."

Chevrolet also innovated in the early use of sponsored celebrity programs with the introduction of the "The Dinah Shore Show," which was later renamed, "The Dinah Shore Chevy Show." The program introduced America to one of the iconic taglines of the 20th century, "See the USA in your Chevrolet," which Shore sang at the end of her shows.

Throughout the 1960s, Chevrolet continued to invest heavily in innovative uses of television, using the theme of entwining the Chevrolet brand and pride in America. A memorable commercial from the period placed a Chevy Impala on top of Utah's iconic Castle Rock. It also pushed beyond the 30/60-second TV spot with 5.5-minute commercials showing travel scenes of the United States.

From this perspective, consumer brands seem to be largely a result of the culture of consumption explosion following the demand for products and services after the Great Depression and World War II. In reality, by that time, Levi's, Coca-Cola, and other brands were nearly a century old. The constant refreshment that advertising gave to brands glowed with a mid-century aura of youth and vitality. These older brands were joined by a pantheon of newly minted ones, which would go on to dominate our kids' point of view, such as the Keebler Elves and McDonald's. They developed to address the unique demands of a more time-pressed and youth-oriented society and continue to change with our increasingly fast- paced culture.

Throughout history, U.S. brands were—and are—uniquely positioned for acceptance by a wide variety of cultures. U.S. ideas and values incorporate global contribution. Ethnic and geographic differences have less of an influence in the United States than in many countries. As the Shift Age pushes us towards an era of global thought, it is a benefit to brands that America, itself, is something of a global brand, and an aspirational idea that can serve as motivation to generations of people. Even recent studies have shown that a significant percentage of most countries' television broadcasting comes from the U.S., and the lifestyle, attitude, and products used in these shows reinforces and communicates the desirability and relevance of American brands.

There's no question that brands permeate our lives. In the developed world, each of us typically receives thousands of brand messages per day. American brands may help consumers outside of the US to mediate the key psychological conflict caused by the increasingly global (e.g., not local culture/traditional) and individually focused (e.g., not family or clan/tribe focused) movements brought about by the forces outlined in *The Shift Age*.

CHAPTER 3

THE STAGES OF TECHNOLOGY AND
HOW THEY AFFECT BRANDS

How Communications Revolutionize Brands

Technology drives changes in the way we communicate, and communication distribution mediums—such as newspapers, broadcast and the Internet—drives brands. The reasoning is simple: in addition to delivering news and entertainment, these media are excellent vehicles for advertising, aka the lifeblood of brands. It follows, then, that advances in media also alter the brand landscape. A glimpse through history illustrates the changing of communication and brands through ancient times, into the Age of Exploration, the Industrial Age, the Information Age and now, the Shift Age.

Today, technology and, therefore, communication, is growing at a rate that's faster and increasingly more rapid than at any other time in history. The theories of advancement and change encompassing technology and communication have enormous implications for the media. Print, broadcast, and the Internet, are, at their core, in the business of information transmission, and are directly impacted by changes in cost of information processing, storage, and distribution. In recent decades, we've seen IT capacity growing exponentially, which has led to the rapid introduction of new media and a rapid decline of once dominant media. This means that advertisers are challenged now, more than ever before, to master new media.

Despite the rapid change that's happening in the transmission, price, form, and structure of media, the industry can be comforted by this fact: the changes occur in a roughly predictable fashion. That brings us back to Moore's Law and The Law of Accelerating Returns of Kurzweil, which by extension suggests that each successive period of dominance of an emerging form of media lasts roughly one half that of its predecessor. The lesson: don't get too comfortable. Mark Twain once said, "If you don't like the weather in New England, wait five minutes." Today, we can apply that brevity to technology and media.

Communication media move through four phases in its life cycle:

1. Disruptive: When a medium is first introduced, it provides a strategic advantage for those advertisers who understand its importance and determine the optimum ways to exploit the new disruptive mode.

2. Dominance: The dominant medium becomes the focus of advertising, and agencies tend to be built around an expertise in managing this media. Advertising campaigns tend to focus on the dominant media, with others used as a supplement.

3. Displacement: In this stage, the once disruptive and then dominant medium begins to experience disruption from a newer medium. The older medium remains a focus of advertiser attention, and may even grow more efficient and profitable as people gain greater understanding of how to optimize advertising for it. At the same time, advertisers focus on emerging media for competitive advantage.

4. Dormant: The medium's importance plateaus. It continues to play a supporting role, and may even morph into a profitable niche, but its role as the central focus of advertising has passed, and a new dominant medium has taken root.

As we apply the life cycle phases to the major forms of media, we can see the disruption-to-dormant pattern is largely influenced by emerging trends in technology, as one mass communications system gives way to the other, creating new strategic opportunities for advertisers. Take a look at the evolution of each major medium:

- Newspapers: This print medium came to dominance through advances in the telegraph, with early industrial production (steam engine printing presses) and railroads providing cheap paper, while also helping concentrate the populations of urban areas. The first major regional and even national distribution of newspaper advertising, combined with national distribution from railroads, helped bring about some of the first major branded products (e.g., Quaker Oats, the first trademark registered in the United States for a breakfast cereal, 1877).

- Radio: This audio medium was brought to dominance through mass electrification and the invention of the vacuum tube (which was the forerunner of the microchip). Radio provided much more intimate, personal, and intrusive advertising than found in newspapers. It enhanced advertisers' abilities to impart emotion and personality to their brands. For example, the first paid radio advertisement was broadcast in 1922, and it marketed a local apartment complex company: Queensboro Corporation in New York City.

- Network television: Technologically, television was a combination of advances built on the infrastructure developed for radio, with an added visual element; sight and motion added to sound. It created a powerful advertising platform for brands to capture attention and create emotional connections with consumers. For example, Tony the Tiger was created in 1951 as the animated spokesman for Frosted Flakes, informing kids everywhere of his love of Frosted Flakes. "They're Grrrrreat!"

- Cable television: The deregulation of broadcast television in the late 1970s and the launch of communications satellites unleashed innovations in cable transmission technology. Cable TV vastly expanded channels and programming, and provided brands with the opportunity to target, more efficiently, viewers with specific tastes, such as CNN (founded in 1980) and MTV (founded in 1981). Remember the song "Video Killed the Radio Star?" It was the first music video broadcast on MTV and forecast the future of one medium (TV/cable) becoming dominant over another (radio).

- Broadband Internet/browser: Broadband Internet was originally developed among science and computer research centers and led to the invention of the web browser, which allowed consumers' access to the Internet. Now, brands could personalize their message to be shared in the most relevant times, in context.

Amazon, for example, which was founded in 1994, uses individual level data to drive suggestive cross selling based on consumer browsing and purchase history.

- Mobile Internet/Social Media: The emergence of mobile Internet and social media, both clearly becoming a force by 2010, is the first time that marketers have had to deal with two separate disruptions simultaneously. With the dawn of both, consumers increasingly share a vast array of personal information, and advertisers are able to target them more accurately than ever before, during all hours of the day and night. Of the two, Mobile may well prove the most disruptive with the emergence of the vast amounts of locational and behavioral information from potentially billions of cellphones, the scope is likely to far outstrip what is generated in social media.

Media	Becomes Distributive	Begins to be Eclipsed	Span of Primary Strategic Advantage	Technology Drivers	Impact on Brands
Newspaper	1850	1920	70 years	Industrial production/ railroads/ telegraph	Birth of modern national consumer brands
Radio	1920	1950	30 years	Mass electrification/ invention of the vacuum tube	Brands gain a "voice" and personalities emerge
Network Television	1950	1980	30 years	Cost reductions in electronic components/ commercialization of television technology	Brands become television characters and even stars
Cable Television	1980	2000	20 years	Deployment of national cable network, compression of data transmission	Start of fragmentation and targeting of "mass" brands
Broadband Internet/ Browser	2000	2010	10 years	Deployment of national broadband network/ commercialization of browser technology	Brands get personal: presented to consumers in specific occasions and settings and to specific audiences
Mobile Internet/ Social Media	2010	2015-2020 (estimate)	5-10 years (estimate)	Deployment of 3G+ national cellular network, rollout of smart phones, growth of social networking sites	Brands become social: travel with consumers in their lives, increasingly engage with consumers

CHAPTER 4

GLOBAL BRANDS

A Global Perspective on Brands

Brands speak volumes about the culture that created them, while acting as magpies, picking up bits and pieces of the influences around them, and transmitting relevant messages back to the consumer. To look back at memorable commercials and advertising campaigns that brands have produced over time and across the world, is to walk away with a unique lesson on history, trends, values, gender, the economy, and so much more. By encapsulating political and economic change in a tasty, easy-to-digest nugget, brands have the power to help people deal with disruptions in their lives and remind them that they are not alone.

If you want to know the dominant theme of a culture, look no further than its largest brands. For example:

- Dominant European brands tend to be about luxury. Examples: Mercedes/BMW out of Germany and Louis Vuitton/L'Oreal out of France. (These brands, along with Ikea and H&M from Sweden, have been making gains in recent years.)

- Dominant Asian brands tend to be Japanese, or, to a lesser extent, Korean, and communicate technological progress and a modern global aesthetic. Examples: Toyota, Honda, Canon, Sony, Nintendo, Panasonic from Japan and Samsung, and Hyundai of South Korea.

- Dominant U.S. brands tend to be about expression of individual freedom and gratification (e.g., the American Dream). Examples: Budweiser, Apple, Coca-Cola, McDonald's.

While Asian countries are huge consumers of brands, they have produced relatively few global brands. Most of the small gains this geographic region has had come from Japanese and South Korean brands.

And then, there is China. Despite the historical and epic economic advances of China, the country has failed to produce a single global brand of any significance. The two Chinese brands that are cited as possible emerging global brands are Tiger Balm and Singapore Airlines. Yet, both brands are actually from ethnically Chinese people living in a former part of Malaysia, in the former British colony of Singapore.

Why has China become such a large consumer of brands but failed to produce its own significant global brand? It could be a simple matter of timing, and eventually we will see Chinese brands of global significance evolve. China is a global leader in economic growth, and it is in the midst of its own industrial revolution. But, it is clearly going through a different pattern of growth than the United States. At the commencement of its own industrial revolution, the United States produced remarkably notable brands, such as the aforementioned Ivory, Coca-Cola, Quaker Oats, and more, which continue to play a role on the world's stage.

The core barrier that China may be experiencing, in terms of producing a global brand, is that Chinese society as a whole has yet to form its own brand—i.e. a meaningful and differentiated position as a culture. *New York Times* columnist David Brooks penned a column exploring this topic in May 2013 ("The Romantic Advantage"), which summed up the reasons aptly:

> Brand managers who've worked in China say their executives tend to see business deals in transactional, not relationship terms. As you'd expect in a country that has recently emerged from poverty, where competition is fierce, where margins are thin, where corruption is prevalent and trust is low, the executives there are more likely to take a short-term view of their exchanges.

But, if China is ever going to compete with developed economies, it'll have to go through a series of phase shifts. Creating effective brands is not just thinking like a low capitalist, it is more so. It is an entirely different mode of thought.

The other emerging commercial giant, India, has much like China, struggled to produce a global brand. The most recognized Indian brand, to date, is the Nano automobile, which is a mini car starting around $2,000 that even Indians have yet to truly embrace. In writing about the Nano, *Car and Driver* said, "Americans will likely prefer a Ford Pinto to the Nano." Ouch.

Brand consumption is in its early stages within India, making it an interesting case study. Significant disposable income did not emerge in the country until the 1990s, and substantial restrictions on global brands and on local conglomerates have limited the adoption rate of the branded merchandise. Before the inflow of foreign brands, there was essentially a monopoly on most products (e.g., one brand of soap for the low end and one brand for the high end). But, times are changing. Today, as India transforms into a more service-led economy, Indian business are steadily becoming brand savvy, and branding as a corporate discipline is catching on quickly.

In fact, Indian trademark applications increased by 64 percent from 2004- 2009. As awareness and acceptance rises, foreign brands are making progress with an increasing brand conscious consumer base. The growing acceptance of brands in India shows a textbook-style adherence to the historic rise of brands: changing demographics and economics coupled with improved connectivity, market liberalizations and higher competition results in a growing reliance on product reputation.

There is no question that brands permeate our lives. In the developed world, each of us typically receives thousands of brand messages per day. Of those, American brands make up the majority of the messages, worldwide. According to Interbrand, the world's largest brand consultancy in 2013, U.S. brands dominated 67 percent of all brands, globally.

American brands may help mediate the key psychological conflict caused by the increasingly global (e.g. not local culture/traditional) and individually focused (e.g. not family or clan/tribe focused) movement brought about by the forces outlined in *The Shift Age*. Consumers can use U.S.-based brands and experience a piece of this new global/ individual focused culture, while still living other parts of their lives in the traditional/family/clan-oriented lifestyle of their local culture.

Brand Equity by Geographic Region
Source: Interbrand

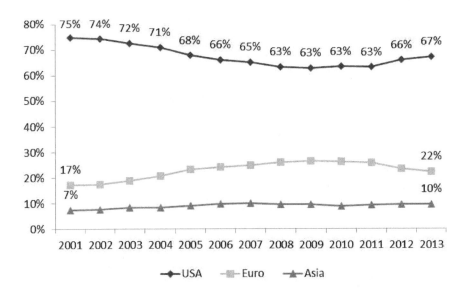

While the overall trend leaves American brands in the clear lead, the traction enjoyed by Samsung, both in the estimate of brand value as well as acceptance of a premium product competitive with Apple, suggests a possible strengthening of the global/pan national esthetic pioneered by Japanese brands. The only two non-U.S. brands of the top ten brands in the Interbrand ranking are Samsung and Toyota. Despite this strengthening, the U.S. brands continue to sustain their historical advantage.

CHAPTER FIVE

THE THREE FORCES OF THE SHIFT AGE

In his first book, *The Shift Age*, published in 2007, David introduced to the world the new age we have entered. Later, with *Entering the Shift Age*, published in 2013, he provided an expanded and deeper look into what is proving to be one of the most transformative times in history. Intrigued by the book, Owen Shapiro helped develop consumer market-research studies based on concepts in *The Shift Age*. These studies not only verified new ways to look at and categorize consumer behavior, but also provided a new way to analyze consumer buying and communications.

Primary among these concepts were the Three Forces of the Shift Age, which underlie most of the changes humanity is now experiencing, and certainly the changes occurring in brands and marketing. We now take a look at the Three Forces of the Shift Age.

Three Forces of the Shift Age

Every age is ushered in by a confluence of forces that disrupt and alter society. The primary force of the Agricultural Age—agriculture—changed how humans lived in terms of diet and created the concept of Place as well as the beginnings of society and civilization. The early forces of mechanization—the invention of the steam engine—and centralization of the Industrial Age drove urbanization, triggering the rapid growth of cities around the world. These also created the hierarchical management structures for business that had only existed in the military until then. This change led to management and management theory, and to the concept of the "job." In the mid-20th century, the forces of subsidized higher education, satellites, and the rapid spread of increasingly powerful computers throughout the world initiated the Information Age.

The phasing is similar with the Shift Age, which is being created and shaped by three major forces:

- The Flow to Global
- The Flow to the Individual
- Accelerating Electronic Connectedness

Of course, there are many other dynamics and influences affecting humanity today, but these three forces are the dominant ones reshaping humanity in the Shift Age. Most of the disruptive changes and the disorienting speed of change we are all experiencing can be traced back to these three forces. It seems as if almost every aspect of human life is in some sort of shift.

This is certainly the case with the communications, advertising, and marketing industries. Since the early days of the Shift Age, in the middle of the first decade of this century, just think of the multitudes of change people in these industries have faced. There have been more disruptive changes and shifts of behavior in the last ten years than in any other ten-to twenty-year period in the history of marketing.

Let us take a closer look at these three forces.

The Flow to Global

The end of the Cold War and the collapse of the Eastern Bloc created the opening for globalism to take root, launching a rapid growth of the global economy. The coming together of Eastern and Western thought created a more unified and integrated way for humanity to think and live. The move from hierarchies to networks flattened corporations and allowed them to move outward horizontally. Global supply chains were developed. All of this new globalism swelled into the force known as the Flow to Global.

Today in the Shift Age, humanity is heading toward a new global integration. As history has unfolded, we have moved through several geographical stages in how we identify our place relative to others: family, tribe, village, city, state, and country. Now, due to our sheer numbers and increasing electronic connectedness, humanity has arrived at a point where a majority of the people on the planet can consider themselves part of one global community.

This is a new phenomenon. Even in the latter part of the twentieth century, we often used the word "international" rather than "global." Today, the words "foreign" and "international" have given way to the word "global," and we find ourselves integrating this new emerging sense of global citizenship with our past identities.

Why and how did this happen? First, there are so many more people today. The global population has increased 75 percent since the beginning of the Information Age in the early 1970s. This population explosion means people no longer feel as though they live far apart from other groups of people, and more of us than ever are clustered in dense population areas we call cities, which are ideal for seeding and fueling economic activity. Along with these economic changes has come a historically unprecedented growth in electronic connectivity, which helped accelerate this new Flow to Global in politics and culture. When the speed of communications accelerated, the world became smaller. Borders opened, boundaries collapsed, and global culture and politics rushed in. For the first time in history, hundreds of millions and then billions of people were exposed to information and opportunity that was global in scope. Distinct national identities started to blur as most nations experienced an increase in multicultural integration.

With all the global economic changes underway and the resultant social changes taking root, people everywhere are now beginning to identify as "global citizens." Whether one has come to this new identity through one's business or line of work, or through political or cultural issues, most of us, to varying degrees, see ourselves as global citizens. Globalization is no longer simply an economic term. It is the name of a force that will course through all aspects of human society for the next ten to twenty years of the Shift Age.

The population growth of the last forty years, the rapidly integrated economy, the issue-led globalization of politics, and the flow of culture around the world via the Internet point us to the next step.

We have entered the global stage of human evolution.

The Flow to the Individual

In the last 30 years, there has been a transfer of power in society from large groups to each person: the Flow to the Individual.

Power has migrated from institutions to individuals due to the explosion of choice, the growth of free agency, the technologies and dynamics moving us from hierarchies to networks, and the ever-increasing electronic connectedness. Gatekeepers are disappearing; disintermediation—and its primary agent, the Internet—is reorganizing the economic landscape. The explosion of choice over the last 40 years shifted power from the producer to the consumer, from the institution to the individual. The individual is becoming the primary economic unit, the micro-micro that is combining with the macro-macro of the Flow to Global. We are distinct individuals who are also global citizens.

This Flow to the Individual can be traced back to the transition in the United States from a production economy that was hierarchical, to a knowledge- and information-based economy that is flat and networked. In today's global marketplace, tens of millions of people have moved from being employees to being independent contractors.

We have increasingly become a culture of free agents. We come together around projects or initiatives, do our work, and then move on to something else. Access to faster wireless high-speed connectivity allows us to work anywhere. This new work reality also means that the work we do, and the people with whom we do it, are often global in scope. Expertise, knowledge, and talent are in demand globally. As free agents with desired competencies, we can offer our services to anyone in the world who might want them, thanks to the electronic connectedness of the planet. This means that the individual is no longer restricted to a specific location or market, but has a much wider geography of possibility and influence.

Ever-increasing choice, ever-increasing connectivity, ever-increasing mobility, and ever-increasing independence from institutional jobs or traditional distribution models are all part of the Flow to the Individual.

Accelerating Electronic Connectedness

The third major force of the Shift Age is the Accelerating Electronic Connectedness of the planet, a recent phenomenon, and also one of the most significant forces in the history of humanity.

Until the latter part of the Industrial Age, entire civilizations, societies, and countries developed in limited geographic spaces. During the course of human history, there were often civilizations in the world that existed simultaneously but were not aware of each other. The Roman Empire, the Mayan Civilization, and some of the greatest dynasties in China existed concurrently—but they had absolutely no knowledge of each other, and therefore developed and imploded in isolation.

The Information Age set the foundation for this profound, but quite recent phenomenon of global connectedness. The Internet did not begin to gain widespread usage until the 1990s, and even then, it was very slow compared to the high-speed and wireless Internet of today. Commercial cellphone use began in the early 1980s, but it took 20 years to go from the first to the billionth cellphone subscriber in 2002. It then took only four years to reach two billion subscribers in 2006, the approximate beginning of the Shift Age. It then took two years to reach three billion cellphone users in 2008, four billion by 2009, five billion by the end of 2010, and 5.3 billion by the end of 2011. As of the writing of this book, there are 7.2 billion people alive today, and approximately 6.1 billion of them have cellphones. If you discount those under the age of eight and those living in remote parts of the world, humanity has now reached almost complete cellphone ubiquity.

Time, Distance, and Place Are No Longer Restrictions

What all of this connectedness means is that for the first time in human history it can be said that time, distance, and place no longer limit human communication. Think about that! In the some 150,000 years that modern humans have lived on earth, only in the last five years has human communication been freed from the limitations of time, distance, and place. Imagine living one- or two-hundred years ago and trying to comprehend communication with another person unconstrained by time, distance, or place. This was not true even at the beginning of the Information Age. It would have been an incomprehensible concept. Yet, it is now our reality—and it is the new reality of brands and the marketing of them.

As of the writing of this book, there are between two and three billion people online, and that number is rapidly increasing. It will increase even faster when the more than four billion people who have cellphones move up to smart phones or other mobile-computing devices.

The Two Realities of the Shift Age

We now live in a broadband, high-speed Internet world.

This means that all of us now have two realities we must manage: our physical reality and our screen reality. The physical reality is the one that has existed throughout history and, until the later stages of the Information Age, was the only "reality." Now, we also have our screen realities. They are both important. How a girl in high school presents herself in the evening on Facebook is every bit as important as how she presents herself the next day at school. Checking, tailoring, and refining our screen realities has become part of our daily routine. It has even become an obsession for some—because our non-physical reality has become just as tangible in many ways as our physical reality.

Physical reality is based upon molecules, while screen reality is based upon digits and electrons. That is why screen reality is evolving faster than the physical reality; it is not nearly as dependent on, or limited by, mass and volume. Thus, screen reality has a competitive advantage over physical reality, and we are beginning to see how that advantage is playing out in the physical world. What is one of the reasons that bookstores and big-box retailers are going out of business? Amazon.com.

These two parallel but co-existing, co-evolving realities represent the underpinnings of all the transformation that is going to happen in marketing and branding over the next century. In a very concrete sense, an entirely new reality has been dropped on brands and those who manage them—and the methods and strategies that worked so well in a one-reality world will not necessarily work in a two-reality world. Sure, television was a screen, but brands used it to provoke an action in physical reality. It was a one-way platform. The Internet, however, is not only a two-way medium, it is an entirely new dimension of human consciousness—one where the communication is no longer one to many; it is all to all.

Summary

When 80 percent of humanity has the capability of connecting with each other, any time, from almost anywhere, it amplifies the Flow to Global, connecting us all for the first time in history. The Accelerating Electronic Connectedness of the planet has provided the technological connectivity for humanity to be as one, all connected to each other.

When any one of us can put out a message or develop content that can be shared—at or near the speed of light—with up to 80 percent of humanity, we each have potential new powers of influence that are no longer limited by place, class, wealth, or institutional power. This

Accelerating Electronic Connectedness places power in the hands of individuals, thus amplifying the Flow to the Individual.

The transformative, powerful Three Forces of the Shift Age have forever changed branding and marketing. Any marketing professional today must have a core understanding of these three forces, as they are the underpinnings of what brands and marketing are and will be during the next 10-15 years.

PART TWO:
CURRENT AND FUTURE TRENDS

CHAPTER 6

KEY TREND – FROM INSTITUTIONAL
TO INDIVIDUAL

One of the significant key trends that has already transformed brands, and the marketing of them, is the shift from Institutional to Individual power. This trend has brought incredible change in the last 15 years, and will continue to do so for the next 15 years, as well. Flow to the Individual is the primary Shift Age force propelling this change, but two other Shift Age forces are powering it as well.

We live in the greatest age of disintermediation in human history. A distant second would be the century after Gutenberg invented the moveable-type press and, in 1455, published the "Gutenberg Bible." Gutenberg's printing press disintermediated knowledge from manuscripts read and interpreted only by religious leaders and the aristocracy, making knowledge much more widely available via the printed book.

The Internet is the primary force of disintermediation today. Whereas the moveable-type press disintermediated knowledge, the Internet will—to a greater or lesser degree—disintermediate almost every aspect of human life.

The centralized, hierarchical structures of the Industrial Age created institutional distribution models for all the inventions that occurred during that era. The institutional distribution models of the newspaper and broadcast industries were based upon scale, and were corporate in structure. For decades, there were only a few entities sending out information and programming in a one-way, one-to-many model. This model existed until the last decade of the 20th century, when the dynamics of the Information Age and the early roots of the Shift Age radically disrupted this marketplace dynamic.

Up until this time, brands came from corporations. These corporations marketed various brands through the distribution channels of other corporations. People said they worked on a brand,

and were part of the hierarchical brand team of the institution. Brands, too, were institutional. Now we live in the age of the personal brand—the brand of Me. "What is your brand?" is such a common question now that, even in school, teachers encourage students to think of themselves as a brand.

Up until the 1990s, the centralized institutional distribution channels of major brands operated in a highly structured, scheduled, and controlled environment. Big-city newspapers full of advertising came out in the morning and in the afternoon. Television networks dictated the schedule of shows. Costs of production and distribution were high, and the cost of entry into these distribution models was extremely high. Therefore, brands and media distribution were all powerful and in full control. How quaint that now sounds!

Any marketing professional over the age of 40, and in the work force today, understands this has occurred [*Joe, remember when we controlled our brand message and when it went out? Ah, the good old days when it was simple; we were in control!*] The question is, where do we go from here?

Well, first let's take a look at the profound changes already wrought by the Internet's disintermediating power:

Scheduled delivery of content	-> Always available and on-demand
Institutional control of content	-> Individual control of content
One-to-many information flow	-> Many-to-many information flow
Scale	-> Fragmentation -> Atomization
Physical	-> Non-Physical
Place based	-> Space based, any place
Control	-> No control

One simple way to see into the future is to accept and plan for continuing movement from the left to the right above. Technology and ever faster, more widespread connectivity will ensure this flow.

Just think about the dominant dynamic today of the flow to mobile. The mobile screen is not only in ascendancy in the general society, it is already triumphant with the younger generations. Companies that until very recently dominated the PC world, and then the laptop world, are struggling to make the transition to mobile. The disruption has been too fast for them to keep up, so they are falling behind. Today, the Internet is the connective tissue of communications, and the technologies associated with it will continue to drive control to the individual user—the person with a screen in their hand.

Relationship Marketing

The first-stage thinking about this evolution led to the concept of relationship marketing. Since communication is now two-way, it has become a "relationship" between the brand and the consumer. While this is true, it is already a dated concept. The 'relationship' stage will, of course, be where many consumers will stay. For the majority, it will be simply a transition phase, because the power of the Flow to the Individual is also giving way to the power of the collective—which is nothing more than the power of individuals who can share an idea and act on it.

With regard to what the future may bring for brands and marketing, the almost obsessive use of the phrases "relationship marketing" and "consumer engagement" suggest that they are mature, if not exhausted, ideas. They are certainly valid and real, but they are mainstream ideas that will soon lose their potency.

Individual Brands

When individuals could connect globally via the Internet, the cost of entry to being a brand collapsed. Bloggers developed brands from their kitchens. People with digital cameras created branded channels on YouTube. Social media allowed people to create brands from anywhere using only their fingers and thumbs.

Institutional brands still exist, of course, and will continue to exist in the foreseeable future. It's just that institutional brands are no longer exclusive, and certainly no longer in control. Yesterday, there were hundreds of institutional brands. Today, there are millions of institutional and personal brands. New ones are being developed every day, by anyone who has an idea, connectivity, and a smart phone.

CHAPTER 7

KEY TREND – ASCENDANCY OF WOMEN

One of the most significant trends of the Shift Age is the ascendancy of women. In the years to come, there will be a greater alteration in the view of gender, and in the equalization of women with men, than in any prior age. When the Shift Age gives way to the next age, one of the clear historical realities will be how our entire view of gender has been transformed, making previous inequalities look as antiquated as a corset is now.

This trend is due, in large part, to the great flow toward equality for women that occurred during the Information Age, which coincided with the women's liberation movement of the 1970s. The Information Age created a knowledge economy, which relied less on the sort of brute physical strength that drove the Agricultural and Industrial Ages.

In the 1970s, women began to rightfully demand equality and proceeded to fight their way into all forms of institutions that had either excluded them or greatly limited their participation: corporations, private clubs, the military, universities, and the sciences. Title IX became law in 1972, creating equality in all levels of education, most famously in athletics. By the 1980s, when it became clear that we were in the Information Age, the landscape of gender equality had been forever altered, and fundamental change moved throughout the developed countries of the world.

Think of a fifty-year arc from 1975 to 2025, from the beginning of the Information Age to the zenith of the Shift Age. View this arc as the trajectory of women in all aspects of society. As this book is being written, we are a bit more than 80 percent of the way through this fifty-year passage. Think of all the change that has occurred in this time, particularly when looked through the longer lens of history. However, this amount of change will be easily met and surpassed by the remaining 20 percent to 2025. The amount of power that women will gain, in almost every area of human endeavor in the next twelve years, will match, and probably exceed, their gains over the last thirty-eight years.

There are many signs that clearly point to this ascendency of women. In higher education, the majority of graduates are women, particularly in developed countries. The old hierarchical management models are giving way to more horizontal net-like structures, spreading power more evenly. The continuing flow of power from physical reality to screen reality further separates one's economic potential from their physical strength. Finally, as the older generations—baby boomers, the silent generation, and even genXers—yield power to the younger generations, for whom gender equality is pretty much a birthright, the last barriers to true equality will disappear, as will the antiquated thinking of the past.

So, the ascendency of women will continue due to several dynamics:

- There are still inequalities that need, and eventually will, be erased.

- Screen reality is gender neutral; fewer physical inequalities or gender distinctions will exist on the screen reality than have in physical reality.

- Structures and hierarchies will give way to nets and nodes.

- The views of Millennials and Digital Natives, raised in a world of greater gender equality, will replace those of their parents' generations, which grew up in a more gender-unequal world.

- Female college graduates will continue, at least in the near term, to outnumber male graduates.

The ascendency of women in the Shift Age is not a battle of the sexes won by women, and should not be looked at this way. Rather, it is an extremely significant evolutionary step in the history of both sexes. Many of the social, physical, and cultural forces that have defined men and women since the beginning of the Agricultural Age are in dramatic shift. Historians in the future will look back at the Information Age as the seeding and the beginning of these shifts. These future historians will view the Shift Age as the first age of humanity when women finally and fully shared in the shaping of history.

Obviously, brands and marketing will be affected. Let's take a look at some of the possible impact this shift toward women will have.

Shifts and Changes

In the long history of brands, men have dominated marketing to both men and women. As the fields of market research and demographics developed in the second half of the 20th century, men increasingly marketed a majority of brands to women; research showed that women buy most of the goods in a nuclear household.

In the past two decades, this dynamic has changed as the social, cultural, and economic landscape evolved. Two-income families meant gender roles were changing. Women were no longer at home to watch daytime soaps, which were a lucrative advertising vehicle. Men became more involved with the household and with the raising of children. More women watched sports. More women were involved in business. More men stayed at home or worked from home. Most of the rules about gender marketing had to change, and they did. Gender-based demographics gave way to more nuanced psychographics.

Of course, many brands are distinctly targeted to separate genders, and that will continue. But, in most cases, mere gender is no longer a useful market differentiator. Increasing granularity of digital media now allows individuals to be targeted based upon their behavior in the screen reality— which is much more nuanced and revealing. In the future, messaging will become increasingly individualized, based on ever more sophisticated analyses of exponentially larger reams of personal data. This transformation will not only decrease the importance and wisdom of gender-based marketing, it will require marketers to be much more imaginative and strategic in their messaging.

As women gain equality and power in the marketing world, they will be more willing to try new ideas and to explore new ways of doing things. They will no longer need to show they can succeed in 'a man's world,' and instead will develop new outlooks based on the marketplace becoming 'an individual's world.' Just the fact that equality has occurred, will free women from holding on to legacy marketing strategies and beliefs created by men. Everything will be challenged. Marketing campaigns will become relationships to humanity. In the digital world, brands can be nurtured and tweaked until they find their audience and their customer base.

It is difficult, without sounding a bit sexist, to predict the profound changes on the horizon in a world where women are ascendant. Perhaps the word "sexist" itself will fall into disuse. What is clear, though, is that women will increasingly run brands and marketing. Already, women are building and managing brands for a female audience. The increase in social media will only reinforce this trend, since women typically dominate social media, particularly those that are most valuable in supporting brands such as Facebook, Twitter, and Pinterest.

CHAPTER 8

KEY TREND – SHIFT AGE GENERATIONS

The Shift Age is and will be a time of great generational transfer of power, influence, and authority. In this, the second decade of the 21st century, we are about to start one of the greatest and fastest generational transitions in history.

It must be said at the outset that looking at the world through the lens of generations can be somewhat limiting. Loose generalizations and blanket assumptions about tens of millions of people don't do justice to the full range of individuality and uniqueness that's actually represented in any given generation. That said, as we look ahead to the future of brands and how they are marketed, it is important to understand the younger generations coming into the marketplace. Their behavior, as consumers and people, is and will be different from that of prior generations.

In his book, *Entering the Shift Age*, David called the Millennials and Digital Natives "the Shift Age Generations," as they will largely shape the age.

Millennials

- were born between 1981 and 1997.
- are innovating technology and communications.
- will invent new patterns, structures, and ways of thinking.

Digital Natives

- were born since 1997.
- were born into the information-overloaded, hyper-connected world.
- will lead to new level of consciousness.

Millennials

Much has already been written about the Millennials. They have been endlessly analyzed, criticized, and judged by older generations. There is always a trap, when one generation analyzes another, as generational biases are often deeply embedded in the analysis. What is clear, is that the Millennial Generation is already changing the world.

Their connectedness, their collaborative ways of engagement, their impatience and need for constant feedback and their civic-mindedness are creating new ways of looking at life and work. The older part of the Millennial Generation is now beginning to assume positions of power, and will continue to do so in this decade. Waves of innovation in the technology and communications sectors are being led by this incredibly dynamic generation, and they are inventing new approaches to just about everything.

The greatest demarcation of this generation is technological. It can be segmented into two groups, those born between 1981 and 1991, and those born between 1991 and 1997. The older group moved through the early stages of Internet connectivity, whereas the younger group stepped into connectivity when it was high speed and wireless. The older generation had significant experience with early-generation cellphones, without Internet connectivity, before moving on to smart phones and then app phones. The younger group often had a smart phone as their first phone.

The Millennials will be the first new adult generation of the Shift Age and the 21st century. As they move into their place in society, the workplace, and global culture, they will dramatically accelerate the collapse of legacy thinking and will initiate magnitudes of change in all areas of life. Their thinking, behavior, morals, and world view will be ascendant over the next two decades. They will reach upper levels of organizational power in the late 2010s and the 2020s, when the first of their generation will become leaders of national politics, multinational organizations, and cultural and nonprofit organizations. This of course means they will be leaders of brands and leading decision makers in the world of marketing. In fact, due to the long history of youth in the advertising business, the Millennials are already a significant force on both the creative and consumer sides of brands and marketing today.

Millennials also are more plugged into Shift Age power, which is influence. Power in prior ages was largely based upon control; someone—some party, some company—wants to control this country, this market, this company, this relationship. That kind of controlling power will still exist, of course. In the Shift Age, however, the ability to influence is the new ascendant power. In their collaborative, networked behavior, Millennials instinctively embrace this new reality. They want to influence ideas, design, behavior, and different ways of looking at the world—and they are bringing this energy and desire into the marketing profession.

These are some of the key attributes this generation brings to the future of brands and marketing that are distinctly different from their elders.

- They have matured with less gender and racial bias.
- They have grown up with a much more global sense of themselves.
- They are much more collaborative and collective in their thinking.
- They come into adulthood at a time of great economic hardship.
- They seek to influence more than control.

All of these differences from the Baby Boomers and GenXers are profound, particularly when you think about how brands will be marketed in the future.

Digital Natives

The Digital Natives are the first generation born into the digital landscape. They have never experienced a time without the Internet, mobile phones, or high-speed wireless connectivity. [People over the age of 35—who comprise most of the power infrastructure in brands and marketing today—are digital immigrants, having come to these technologies in adulthood.] They have matured with Search as a reality and immediate option. As they age, most of the world's knowledge and information is just a few keystrokes away. They are the first generation born into a fully developed screen reality, or the reality of no-placeness. They are the first generation that has been able to instantaneously communicate with anyone, anyplace in the world—practically for free.

Another way of thinking about the Digital Natives is that they are the first generation born into the busy, hyper-connected world of information-overload. Though they do not necessarily feel overloaded. It is the only world they have known. Parents of Digital Natives have all seen this with their children. They can sit with the television on, connected to the Internet, maintaining multiple text conversations while listening to music on their ear buds. No stress, just hyper-processing of incoming and available data. Compare that to the digital immigrants of the Boomer or GenXer generations, who have grown up feeling the pressure of information overload, and stress out in managing it all. Older generations, the ones who have shaped brands and the marketing of them, predominantly grew up in an analog world where connections existed— via letters, phone, and the early Internet—but were nowhere as robust, instantaneous, or as voluminous as they are now. As a result, of all this informational input, the Digital Native's brain is wired to work differently. Go ahead, ask your ten-year-old daughter how she is doing with information overload. She will look at you with a blank face and wonder what you are talking about. A state of constant "overload" is simply reality for her.

The Digital Natives are the first generation of the 21st century. Born since 1997, they have no real memories of the last century. This means that all the rules, issues, plans, events, doctrines, and legacy thinking of the 20th century are practically ancient history to them.

The Digital Natives, as with the Millennials, can be broken down into two groups, again based upon technology, those who were born between 1997-2009, and those born since 2010. Think about what has happened with connectivity and technology just since 2010.

- Touchscreens have become the norm.
- Global cellphone connectivity has crossed 70 percent.
- Tablets have become ubiquitous, starting with the iPad in 2010.
- App phones – iPhones and Android phones have achieved market dominance in the United States.
- 3G has rapidly given way to 4G high-speed wireless connectivity, which has become commonplace in many countries.
- eBook readers have taken off in the United States, and eBooks as a percentage of books sold have significantly increased.
- DVDs have given way to streaming.
- Smart music-subscription platforms, such as Pandora and Spotify, have grown dramatically.

So, in a middle-class or upper-middle-class household in 2013, a Digital Native will consume most content on interactive screens. This younger part of the generation will, therefore, never remember content that wasn't on a screen—unlike their parents, who can remember content in physical forms such as books, CDs, and DVDs.

Think about a three-year-old using an iPad today. How will that child view the world as a 20-year-old? It boggles the mind to think about how different her view of the world, and her place in it, will be. Indeed, Digital Natives will grow up in ways no generation ever has. They will be the generation that will lead us, guide us, and help usher us into new realms of creativity and consciousness.

How will they select and integrate brands into their lives? What qualities of brands will appeal to them? How will marketers influence them? Or, taking a slightly longer view, how will they recast, reinvent, and reinvigorate marketing?

In the next three chapters, we look at three trends that will profoundly shape marketing in the years and decades ahead. Please keep the qualities and attributes of the Millennials and Digital Natives in mind when reading the following *Brand Shift* chapters. These will be trends they intuitively understand, embrace, and continue to integrate into in their lives.

CHAPTER 9

KEY TREND - THE SCREEN REALITY AND
THE RAPIDLY GROWING NEUROSPHERE

In Part One of this book, we gave a brief overview of various dynamics of the Shift Age. We discussed the fact that in this second decade of the 21st century, most people live in two realities, the physical reality and the screen reality. The physical reality is our existence in the material world, while the screen reality is the alternate world that exists in digital space, and is accessible through the screens on our various devices. The physical reality is based upon atoms and molecules while the screen reality is based upon electrons and digits.

We also discussed how the screen reality is morphing or evolving faster than the physical reality. This means that the screen reality is actually changing our physical realities. Amazon, for instance, is triggering change to the physical landscape of retailing. The Internet is diminishing all forms of physical content—such as newspapers, books, CDs, and DVDs—and replacing it with online systems of storage and delivery.

Increasingly, this screen reality is becoming the repository of our lives. We keep our contacts, communications, calendars, photos, videos, music, and transactional records online or "in the cloud." It could be said that much of the physical reality—at least relative to human interactions, consumption, and documentation—is being sucked into the screen reality. This is not an exaggeration, since so much of the activity that we use in the physical world—communication, socializing, reading, research, shopping, entertainment, even medical care—is now conducted through our screens.

This means that brands and marketing are increasingly driven by, and contained within, our collective screen reality. The future of marketing and brands will continue to flow in the direction of screen reality, and will expand along with its growing influence and ubiquity. Sure, we will still be buying food, driving cars, and doing the dishes in physical space. Sure, marketing messages will reach us in physical space. Sure, we will still gather socially in physical places. The fundamental difference today is that the physical reality is beginning to take a back seat to the emerging screen reality in terms of relevance to our daily lives.

It has been said that the Internet is to the future of reality what the Model T was to automobiles, or what early black-and-white television was to today's large-screen LCD TVs. Well, if we are only ten years into high- speed global connectivity, it's not difficult to predict that screen reality is in its infancy, and that it will only grow in importance. That's a given.

After all, the Treo and Blackberry phones were the screen reality of hand- held devices ten years ago. Compare that to the current reality of touch- screen app phones and tablets today. In a few years, having a hand-held device may well be optional or irrelevant, since glasses, ear buds, watches, and clothing will soon be able to perform all the same functions. Thus, technology will continue to disrupt the status quo. The one element these devices will have in common is they will connect people to the screen reality. That's where much of the future of brands will unfold.

An easy way to think of this bicameral sense of reality, and how we experience it, is to define these two realities as physical space and digital space or digispace. This is a word we have coined. We think it more clearly reflects the new digital screen reality than a word like cyberspace.

New times and new thinking provoke the creation of new words. We offer up *Digispace* and the larger concept of the *Neurosphere*.

The Neurosphere

Neurosphere is a word that we—particularly David in his writing and talks around the world—have used for years. If the biosphere is where life can exist, think of the Neurosphere as the place where thought can exist. The Neurosphere is, in fact, the extension and collective aggregation of *all* human thought. It is the technical extension of all human neurological activity, and it exists both in our minds and in the screen reality that is evolving through and around us.

Think of the Neurosphere as the synaptic, pulsating, connective, ever expanding other-world where our communications, entertainment, knowledge, transactions, and social interactions reside. The Neurosphere is where leading-edge, on-going transformative and evolutionary change for humanity will largely occur over the next 20 years. It is, in fact, a technology-based model for the next evolutionary shift in human consciousness.

Think back to the last chapter about the Shift Age Generation, particularly the Digital Natives. This generation will be the first to fully live their entire lives connected to the Neurosphere. It is where they find grandma, games, information, friends, and entertainment to watch. They will experience the Neurosphere as a wholly integrated part of their single reality, since the physical reality and screen reality never collided in their lives. *Online* and *offline* are words they will not understand. [*What line mommy? Where is the line on or off?*]

This Neurosphere is the new space of humanity in the 21st century, but until now, it has only existed as an idea. Almost 90 years ago, French philosopher Teilhard de Chardin theorized about the continued evolution of human consciousness in his work *Phenomenon of Man*, calling the ever-greater integration and unification of human consciousness the "Noosphere." What de Chardin, other visionary philosophers, and many science-fiction writers described is now the new reality in which we live—and where the future of brand marketing will unfold.

CHAPTER 10

KEY TREND – MEMES TO MOVEMENTS, INFORMATION FLOW TRANSFORMING INTO SOCIAL CHANGE

Though the Neurosphere is an extension of humanity's thought and knowledge, it operates with profoundly different dynamics than the physical reality and old media of the last century.

First, of course, is the difference between physical content delivery and digital delivery. Only a few decades ago, most media was distributed physically. Newspapers and magazines were printed on paper. Market research was done via mail and the landline phone. Even television and radio were distributed via tapes sent to stations or networks, which then distributed them using physical broadcast and microwave towers. Digital files are smaller and faster to transmit. Faster, in part, due to fiber-optic connectivity, wherein data moves around the world at the speed of light. Sending files to the other side of the world does not take much longer than sending files to your next-door neighbor.

Second, information moves much more quickly across a connected network than across or through separate, distinct distribution channels. The Internet **is** the distribution for and connective tissue of media, content, and marketing for the foreseeable future. It provides global, moment-to-moment connectivity for both marketers and consumers, allowing virtually everyone, everywhere to travel around in Digispace at the speed of light.

Third, the Internet and the Neurosphere are interactive. Anyone with a connection can interact with any other person with a connection. This means that there is a synaptic, catalytic dynamic to the Neurosphere that is unprecedented in human history. Messages can change nature and form as millions of people interact with them, and the power of that message can grow exponentially larger as more people view it.

Fourth, this is exploding rapidly. With the ongoing development of smart environments that record data and track behavior and events, we are now integrating the Internet of Things into the existing Internet of people. We will look at this more deeply in the following chapter, Big Data.

Memes

Think of a meme as an idea, or thought, or aspect of social behavior that rapidly moves through a culture or society. Memes have existed for a long time, but the dynamics of Digispace allow them to move much faster through the cultural consciousness of the Neurosphere. There are no physical boundaries to contain them, so they can easily spread throughout the world.

The word "meme" was coined by the British scientist Richard Dawkins at the beginning of the Information Age. He defined meme as:

"An idea or element of social behavior passed on through generations in a culture, especially by imitation."

and

"A cultural item that is transmitted by repetition in a manner analogous to the biological transmission of genes."

In the past, memes often showed up as fads. Hula hoops, Teenage Mutant Ninja Turtles, cabbage-patch dolls, pet rocks, the Rubik's Cube, dance crazes such as line dancing or the Macarena—all of these are examples of memes that took hold of the popular imagination for a time. Advertising jingles or slogans could be meme-like. "Reach out and touch someone," "You wonder where the yellow went," "See the USA in your Chevrolet," "Where's the Beef?" In a controlled media environment, Madison Avenue had the power to create memes almost at will. And, getting to this level of social saturation was how advertisers measured success.

In the hyper-connected present and future world of the Neurosphere, memes may actually be more important and powerful—but they can also take on a life of their own. No one controls them—they just materialize.

In early 2012, David wrote a blog column titled, "Memes to Movements," about the Occupy Wall Street movement.

> In the Shift Age, there is a new, rapid reality of Memes to Movements. Think about Occupy Wall Street. As I wrote in a recent column, the Occupy movement went from some 75 people demonstrating in a small park in Manhattan to tens of thousands of people demonstrating in hundreds of cities in 80 countries. In one month! That is something that has never happened in human history.

Before September 2011, if someone said "Occupy" to you, you would ask for clarification. Today, that word has meaning. It has become a meme. "We are the 99%" is now a meme. The power of the Occupy and 99%/1% memes are so global and so powerful now because they are both memes and movements.

Now, take a step back and look at the phenomenon of Occupy Wall Street not through the socio-political lens you probably viewed it, but from a marketing perspective. Starting on a single day, 9/17/11, some 75 people first showed up at a small park in lower Manhattan to *occupy Wall Street*. Within days, the initial chanting of "We are the 99%" quickly became a meme about looking at society as the very wealthy 1% versus the rest of the population of 99%. One month later, an estimated 100,000-plus people demonstrated in more than 2,500 cities in 83 countries, "occupying" these respective cities. In all locations, the 99/1 meme was chanted. In less than 30 days, 75 people in one location chanting a slogan grew by 1,333% to 100,000+ in 2,500+ locations—nice growth from a marketing viewpoint.

The mainstream media, thinking that Occupy was a political movement, deemed it largely a failure because no organization or political party emerged from it. This was and is legacy thinking. Why?

One year later, the 2012 Presidential campaign between President Obama and Mitt Romney occurred. What was a significant platform that framed the campaign? That America was ever more economically divided, with the top 1% getting wealthier relative to the 99%. Obama used this 99/1 meme to paint Romney as the 1%. In a participatory democracy of one person/one vote, Obama was happy to cater to 99% of the population.

The 99/1 meme that the Occupy movement created in the fall of 2011 was in fact the context that shaped the U.S. presidential campaign a year later. That is influence! Even if there are no more Occupy demonstrations, the Occupy Wall Street demonstrations created one of the most powerful memes in the world today. Hundreds of millions, if not billions of people now, to some degree, have a 99/1 view of the world.

The subtext of the Occupy Movement and its successful launch of the 99/1 meme is that those who participated refused to develop a hierarchy, or a list of issues or demands. It maintained a leaderless, flat shape that perfectly matched the medium that it utilized, the Internet and social media. The initial inability of mainstream media to understand this amorphous type of organizational structure, with its multiple issues and lack of leaders, is a perfect metaphor for traditional marketing and branding, meeting the new reality of marketing in the Neurosphere. Hierarchies have given way to networks. Authorities have given way to groups. Brand strategy has given way to viral memes. Authority is us, not you.

Perhaps the most successful meme/brand of 2012 was "Gangham Style." An obscure South Korean pop star named Psy released a video on YouTube that is the first video to ever reach one billion views—in months! The original video triggered many spoofs and knock-offs, which have aggregated another billion views, all using the same soundtrack of Psy's original. Is there a marketer in the world who would not love to have that viral dynamic attached to its brand?

Think of the meme as one of the new models of marketing of the future. Make your brand or product a meme, and you have your biggest success!

Social Change

The Occupy Movement existed in both the physical and screen realities. It had a clear physical presence that exploded globally due to use of social media. Social media became the tools of revolution in the Arab Spring. Flash mobs, for fun or protest, happen every day around the world. People use social media to create days where residents arrive at a valued local merchant to drive sales, to say thank you. Globally, it is now understood that social media, and the accelerating connectedness of the Shift Age, have created this extension of human endeavor called the Neurosphere—and that activity in this realm creates social change and events that affect real people.

Combine this with the ever-growing importance of conscious capitalism, and a new dynamic has been created for marketing and brands. The Millennial Generation is particularly concerned with buying products from companies that have made significant commitments and statements about making the world a better place. This type of conscious capitalism becomes amplified in the Neurosphere. People will spread the word about initiatives that help people or the planet. This "halo effect" has greater potential than it has ever had due to the ability of the Neurosphere to accelerate and amplify.

In the future, one of the ways for marketers to win big is to create a meme for a brand that promotes truly positive actions taken by the brand.

The Neurosphere represents a technologically-created extension of human thought that is ever expanding and pulsating. It is the technological model or predecessor of a new connected human consciousness. It is in this global consciousness that the future of brands and marketing will exist, live, thrive, or die.

CHAPTER 11

KEY TREND – BIG DATA

Big Data has become a buzzword. In the last few years, it has gone from a predictive description of a coming information explosion to a widely used but misunderstood techno-hipster catch-phrase. This does Big Data a disservice. What's "big" about it is, that it is a profound technological development that will change human behavior and most aspects of human life over the next 20 years, including brand management and marketing.

So let's take a step back and examine why.

The statistics about the explosion of information today are nothing short of incredible. Humanity created a total of between 3 and 12 exabytes of data, depending on various estimates, from the beginning of modern humanity some 150,000 years ago to the year 2003. An exabyte is a million terabytes. By the year 2010, humanity was generating 3 exabytes of data every four days! In 2014, this means that every day, humanity is creating as much information as it created in the last 150,000 years! Is it any wonder we feel a bit of information overload?

In his book, Entering the Shift Age, David developed some estimates of future data creation:

In the year 2010, all of humanity created 1.8 zettabytes of data. A zettabyte is a thousand petabyte's. Here are my estimates for future data creation.

YEAR	DATA AMOUNT
2015	7.5 zettabytes
2020	35 zettabytes
2025	175 zettabytes
2030	750 zettabytes
2035	3000 zettabytes
2040	12,000 zettabytes

These estimates are based upon taking the current rate of dynamic growth that exists now and projecting it forward. There is little reason to think that this rate of growth will slow, and more reason to think that it accelerates. Therefore, the numbers above should be considered conservative projections.

An impressive amount of the recent data explosion is from the exponential growth of the Neurosphere, due to websites, social media, texting, emails, videos, and everything else that has been/is uploaded and downloaded in the screen reality. Each of us creates more data than our predecessors could ever have created, because we now live within the Accelerating Connectedness of humanity.

Going forward, much of the above estimated data explosion will come from the Internet of Things—trillions of smart chips embedded in our infrastructure, machines, appliances, vehicles, clothing, and personal devices, all of which will be communicating with each other. We will be living in an environment of pulsating data, similar to how we are living in an invisible web of radio waves, cellular signals, and TV signals. The difference is that in this environment, everything we do online is recorded somewhere, and is added to both our individual and collective data banks, where it is analyzed by technological systems that grow in sophistication and capability every day.

A simple metaphor for Big Data is to consider it as the third stage of human mapping. The first stage was the mapping of our physical world, the continents and the oceans. The second stage was the mapping of the ways we traversed the land and sea. This third stage of mapping is of our behavior and thoughts. We are entering a time when almost all of human behavior can be mapped, so Big Data can be thought of as real-time anthropology and sociology. In the Shift Age, every type of business and enterprise must expand its data consumption and analysis exponentially; that is the speed at which our new world operates.

Now, there is an entirely new category of professions that are purely data-focused and driven. Millions of data workers with deep data analytical skills will be needed in this decade alone. In marketing, plans and media strategies will change weekly, if not daily, or in some cases hourly. Marketers will be able to respond to, interact with, and motivate their targeted customers moment by moment.

Yes, this does sound overwhelming. Many reading these words can remember when there were annual marketing plans and media plans—when the launch of a brand was built over months of meetings and brainstorming sessions. Sorry. To compete in this new Big Data landscape, one cannot afford to work with yesterday's data when competitors and customers are making decisions based upon information they received today.

One of the smartest business people we know (and in full disclosure, David's partner in a corporate advising business) Ark Rozental, accurately described the Era of Big Data this way.

> The Big Data Era represents a universal challenge of identifying how and what data to use. To survive, organizations will shift priorities to harness this data for patterns and insights that provide opportunities to add value to the bottom line. The best of them will commit their entire organization to the pursuit of data for the sole purpose of elevating the consumer experience at every touch point. The traditional reactive model of analyze and respond, where companies mine historic data to learn how transactions are performed, will give way to predictive analytics and proactive action.
>
> Therefore, getting closer to the individual will be the most important dimension to realize long-term organizational growth strategy in the next five years. We have arrived at a seminal moment in the history of human communication: the point where further vertical acceleration of communication will test the limits of human ability to communicate effectively—the point where communication focus will have to shift from speed and volume to a hyper- focused feeding and nurturing of one's augmented reality times the world

population. This will put Big Data at the center of every industry and field for the coming decades.

It is challenging to overstate how dramatically this unfolding reality will transform the fields of marketing, branding, and advertising.

In the last two chapters, we discussed the Neurosphere and the concept of memes. Perhaps, you can now see why. Big Data will explode the size, density, synaptic power, and potential of the Neurosphere. Brands will flourish or perish in this arena. Memes will become the flashpoints of brand marketing. There will be memes in the era of Big Data that, in a matter of days, will saturate subsets of consumers; memes that will rapidly saturate geographical locations; memes that will explode globally for days, weeks, and maybe months.

Marketers who think Big Data is just another buzzword, and do not work to understand and embrace its potential, may well put their brands and companies at risk of collapse.

Properly looked at, the era of Big Data might well be a new evolutionary stage of brands, marketing, and advertising. Alternatively, to lift an oft- used phrase from media, it is a new Golden Age of Marketing.

Welcome!

PART THREE:
THE FUTURE

CHAPTER 12

THE BII: BRAND INFLUENCE INDEX

The dominant metaphor for understanding the value of brands is that of "equity." Brand equity is similar to a financial asset, but the term itself is an example of legacy thinking that is growing increasingly irrelevant, since "equity" can now be easily undermined and replaced almost overnight.

To help deal with this paradigm shift, the market research firm, Leo J. Shapiro & Associates LLC has developed a new metric to measure brand effectiveness and growth opportunities for brands through a more effective network presence. This new measurement tool is called the Brand Influence Index (BII). In effect, the BII breaks down Maslow's Social and Esteem elements of the brand relationship into a cogent hierarchy that allows marketers to see where they currently stand in their relationship with their customers, and where are they are likely to enjoy the highest amount of value when cultivating a deeper relationship.

The BII takes into account seismic shifts in the consumer brand/media landscape and provides a new metric for understanding consumers' relationship to brands. It shares insights into how effectively brands engage their customers, and considers how well brands bring customers into the process of promoting and communicating about the brand. It also provides a nuanced gradation of *potential* relationships that consumers might have with brands.

The BII labels the strength of a customer's relationship with a brand, with "Devoted" being the highest, and "Disconnected" being the lowest. Obviously, not all brands can, or even should, strive to have a "Devoted" brand relationship like Trader Joe's. But, when a brand knows where it stands, it also learns how it can improve in the eyes of its customers.

The results of our first BII benchmarking study show that marketers have numerous opportunities to incrementally improve their relationships with customers. That could lead to substantial gains in marketing efficiency and, thus, profitability. To do so, they need to focus on:

- The "achievable" over the "desirable," by realizing where they currently stand with their customers.
- Adjacent higher-value relationships that are available to them.
- Tools (media and messages) that are best suited to achieving those goals.

BII distinguishes itself by allowing brands to make incremental improvements in their relationship styles. It helps identify opportunities to raise a brand to a higher-level of engagement with its customers while following the most cost-effective path.

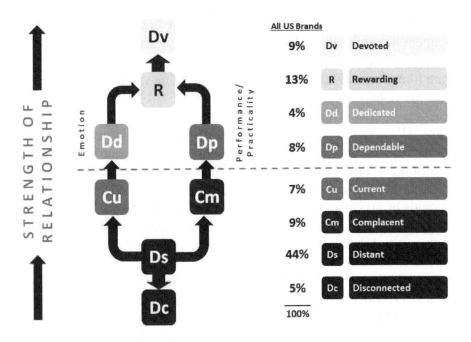

This study examines how 4,000 customers interact with 105 national brands.

Using 200 different measurements, a comprehensive tool was developed that analyzes brand/customer relationships as never before. The data, in part, reveals "Relationship Factors" that quantify consumers' perceptions of various emotional and practicality/performance characteristics of the brand. Other data includes detailed information about the "engagement touch points" through which a brand interacts with customers.

This data is analyzed to provide the marketer a multi-dimensional view of the brand's interaction with its customers, and includes the following.

- The type and strength of relationships, which are grouped into eight distinct types, ranging from least to most engaged with the brand.

- The type and strength of touch points that are engaging the customers.

- The quality and potential value of a customer's loyal behavior.

- The drivers of the brand relationships.

- The marketing activities that can contribute to the relationship.

One particularly powerful use of BII data and analysis is the ability to identify eight key relationships brands can have with consumers. Those include the following:

- Devoted
- Rewarding
- Dedicated
- Dependable
- Current
- Complacent
- Distant
- Disconnected

These clusters provide excellent shorthand for understanding a brand's interactivity with customers. They point toward the specific types of objectives and initiatives that are likely to be necessary and effective.

Brands by BII Relationship

Each of the BII relationships describes a particular set of brands with unique opportunities and challenges.

Devoted: Strongest relationship – brands are a reflection of the consumer; they are not open to alternatives. Key examples include clusters in consumer durables/tech areas.

- Apple
- Toyota
- Google

Rewarding: Strong Relationship – Consumers remain open to alternatives but feel that the brand is bringing them value and has relevance for them. Key examples are inclusive of clusters in the service companies.

- American Express
- Southwest Airlines
- Hyatt

Dedicated: Strong Emotion Driven – High satisfaction and uniqueness, but not seen as really essential or useful. Key examples are reflected in the cluster of 'small indulgence' category.

- Pepsi
- Hershey's
- Vitamin Water

Dependable: Practically driven – brand is seen as traditional and familiar. Key examples incorporate a cluster among less innovative category leaders.

- DQ
- JC Penney
- Smuckers

Current: Moderately strong, emotionally driven – seen as leaders for innovation even if they make consumers sometimes feel self-conscious about using them. Key examples accommodate a cluster in the new 'disrupter' brands.

- Skype
- KIA
- Whole Foods

Complacent: Moderately strong, practically driven – seen as useful/comfortable brands, but customers are not emotionally invested in continued use of the brand. Key examples encompass a cluster in older consumable brands.

- Old Spice
- Dove
- Clorox

Distant: Weak Relationship – brand seen as out of step with consumer/marketplace. Key examples include brands from a variety of categories including:

- Archer Farms
- United
- Twitter

Disconnected: Weakest relationship – brand is seen as market leader, but is abusing its position by not satisfying or rewarding many of its users. Key examples are comprised of larger dominant companies.

- Walmart
- Microsoft
- Facebook

Case Study: the BII of Social Media Brands

To help illustrate the BII approach, we examine a brief case study using leading social media brands Facebook and Twitter. These brands are much more likely than the other 103 brands we studied to have a "Disconnected" relationship with their customers, which is the lowest level of engagement of any of the eight relationship styles identified. It's not that customers think these brands are "bad." In fact, they tend to be viewed as "market leaders" and "up with the times."

These brands, however, are victims of their own success. The value of a social network site can be driven by size. The larger it is, the more valuable it is to use. The "network advantages" of a large social site make its relationship style similar to other highly dominant brands, like Walmart, AT&T, and Microsoft. People use these brands and get value from them, but they just do not feel fully connected to them, because they are considered "too big to love." Somewhat ironically, social media brands are great at building connections between people, but poor at building relationships between their user base and the brands themselves.

Social Media: Poor Relationship, Below Average Engagement

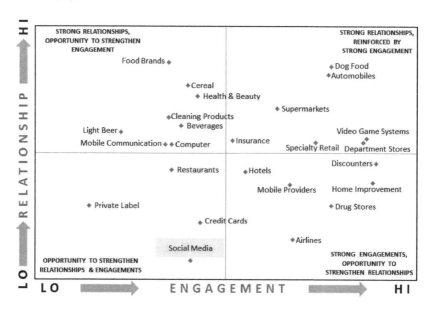

Leading Social Media Brands, Facebook and Twitter, have very poor Relationships and poor Engagements

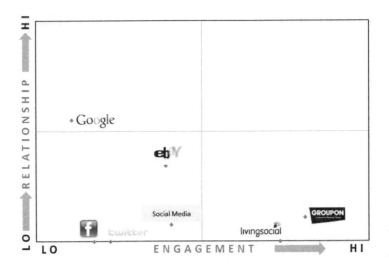

Can social media brands climb the seven steps from "Disconnected" to "Devoted?" Not only is this a tall order, but it probably is also a self-defeating one. Consumers are just not going to find this kind of messaging credible. Social media brands can benefit from small steps forward, garnering a much stronger relationship with their customers by implementing a series of strategic tweaks. In fact, consumers with a "Complacent" relationship to a social media brand are two-and-a-half times more likely to promote and communicate about the brand than those who are "Disconnected."

Social Media: Engagement Improvement Multiplier (EIM)

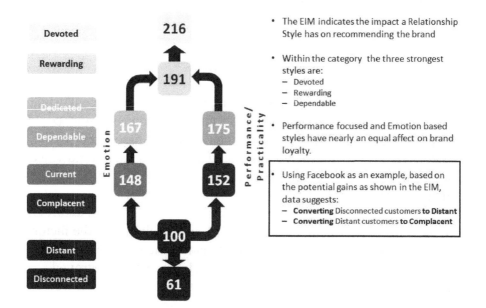

- The EIM indicates the impact a Relationship Style has on recommending the brand

- Within the category the three strongest styles are:
  - Devoted
  - Rewarding
  - Dependable

- Performance focused and Emotion based styles have nearly an equal affect on brand loyalty.

- Using Facebook as an example, based on the potential gains as shown in the EIM, data suggests:
  - **Converting** Disconnected customers **to Distant**
  - **Converting** Distant customers **to Complacent**

The kinds of messages associated with the "Complacent" position, where social media brands fall particularly short, include:

- Not feeling self-conscious about using the brand

- Brand is a good solutions provider

- Brand rewards me for my business

In sum, encouraging consumers to adopt a more "Complacent" style towards their brand, through effective and targeted messaging, could help Facebook and Twitter engage their customer base more effectively. These improvements would strengthen their brand voice and help secure their continued dominance in their respective corners of social media.

In the Shift Age, as hard as it may be to accept, almost all the factors that have constituted successful brand management over the past 50 years are going to be challenged and, to a large extent, destroyed. That doesn't mean brands won't be important—they will. However, the type of legacy thinking and institutional strategies that led to success in the past will no longer work in the future. And, the reason they won't work is that, as the Shift Age unfolds, every individual's relationship to society, government, corporations, markets, the planet, and each other is going to undergo a radical series of transformations that transfer power and influence away from traditional hierarchical structures (where brands have comfortably exerted their authority for decades) to a vast and ever-expanding network of self-organizing nodes guided by shared interests, behaviors, and motivations that are difficult, if not impossible, to predict.

Companies that fail to adapt this new reality will experience the Shift Age as an era of chaos and struggle. Companies that find ways to navigate these uncharted waters, it should go without saying, have a much better chance of surviving and thriving.

The value of the BII—is that it establishes a framework for understanding the different ways in which brands relate to their customers—not in terms of traditional metrics like sales and market share, but in terms of how people develop relationships to specific brands on an emotional/psychological level, and how to start to manage those relationships in an effective way.

If you have read this far, you know that the Shift Age is going to be one of intense hyper-personalization. As people's desires and the technologies to meet them grow ever more sophisticated, people's expectations—particularly regarding the products and services they use—are going to become more intensified, nuanced, and demanding. This is potentially a very good thing for brands like Google and Toyota, which already have a "devoted" following. But, the continued success of such brands is by no means guaranteed. In an age of self-organizing, peer-influenced brand allegiances, customer devotion is going to depend on how well brands cultivate the increasingly intimate relationship they and their customers are going to share. An ever increasing, brand/customer relationship is going to resemble little mini-marriages, where trust, transparency, honesty, communication, and responsiveness are the keys to keeping the relationship viable. Fail in any one of those areas, however, and the relationship will suffer.

Big is not necessarily better in the Shift Age, either. For brands like Walmart and Facebook, which fall into the category of least engagement in the BII index, the combination of their size and disengagement could be catastrophic. As you read this, for instance, it is perfectly within the power of the majority of Walmart's customers to decide, in an instant, to stop shopping there—today. All that would have to happen is for a meme to develop around some aspect of Walmart's business model, and for that meme to show up on a few billion cellphones, sparking a global boycott. It hasn't happened yet, but it easily could. Witness the difficulties Target Corp. is having re-establishing trust with its customers after the data breach that affected more than 100 million of its customers during the 2013 holiday season.

The point is, the BII is a tool that helps companies understand the nature and strength of the psychological/emotional relationship they have with their customers. And, once the parameters of this relationship are defined, the index can be used to guide expectations toward what is possible in terms of change in the future; what is prudent in terms of strategy; and what the outcomes of any given initiative might look like.

Companies that do not consider such information will be flying blind in the Shift Age, wasting their energy and capital looking for a guiding light that isn't there. Then, they will wonder why they keep smashing into walls.

And, we know what happens when things that were once flying suddenly crash into obstacles they can't see.

CHAPTER 13

SOCIAL MEDIA – INTERIM STEP ON THE ROAD TO ALL-TO-ALL COMMUNICATION

Social Media has changed the game for advertisers and marketers over the last 10 years, creating new ways for companies to interact with their customers, deliver messages to ever-more-targeted audiences, and generate various types of viral activity. But social media has also confounded brand managers by wresting control of the narrative away from companies, and giving customers the means to fight back if they feel it's necessary or justified. As marketers well know, the opportunity to interact directly with customers is not always a happy experience. Social media can certainly enhance a brand, but it can also put brand managers on the defensive if unsatisfied customers decide to turn their dissatisfaction into, say, a YouTube video that goes viral.

For those trying to control a message, then, social media is a double-edged sword—one that is about to develop several more sharp and potentially dangerous blades. As much influence as social media has had on marketing, it is just an initial step towards an all-to-all media environment, from which all are learning, and sharing with others. Unfortunately for marketers, this will also be a world in which the idea of "control" over a "message" will soon seem as quaint as a postcard from your grandmother.

In the electronic village, everyone has a soapbox to stand on. People are free to share their opinions, no matter how ill-informed, and there are no barriers to being an author, social critic, food blogger, fashion expert, conspiracy theorist—or futurist, for that matter. The more power individuals gain, however, the less they trust traditional power structures. These are the very structures that have, in the past, prevented them from having the sort of power they now enjoy.

For brand managers, this is an enormous change. Decades ago, consumers respected institutional authority. People bought products because they had been granted the Good Housekeeping Seal of Approval, or had been highly rated by Consumer Reports. Now, people distrust institutions and consult their friends for advice. Research by Leo J. Shapiro & Associates LLC, in 2009, showed that consumers rate online comments from anonymous strangers (social media) as more influential than any form of advertising—simply because such comments are perceived as being more honest. A plumber can advertise all they want, for instance, but without high customers ratings on Angie's List, it won't matter. In the age of social media, the guy with the most "likes" wins.

The result, for brand managers, is that social media has started to pry apart the tightly managed messaging they used to control. Brand managers and marketers must now integrate social media into any brand marketing strategy. All too often, those strategies are created without thinking critically about social media's true usefulness, or recognizing its flaws and limitations.

Crucial to understanding social media as it exists today is the recognition that, for all the impact it has had, it is still very much in the embryonic stages of development. Much of social media's impact has yet to be felt, because the tools currently being used—text messaging, comments, apps, and websites—are crude in comparison to what is coming into the all-to- all Neurosphere, where people's minds, bodies, and emotions will be seamlessly integrated in a way that constitutes an entirely new level of human consciousness.

So far, however, social media has fallen short of its fully disruptive promise in several ways:

- About half of consumers comment on any social media, so the promise of all-to-all communication has really become more-to-all communication. This is better than the few-to-all communication of the broadcast era, but there is a long way to go.

- Much of social media is falsified, generated for a fee for the benefit of client companies. A recent study on Yelp site reviews, for example, revealed that roughly 20 percent of the comments are falsified, even after extensive screening by Yelp to ensure the veracity of comments.

- Social media has been "hijacked," to a large extent by brand marketers who embraced the potential of social media a bit too eagerly. By flooding the Internet with targeted ads, PR campaigns, and other gimmicks, companies trying to connect with "influencers" have inadvertently made their target audience wary and skeptical.

- Many people who use social media platforms actively resist "the pitch," some with enough resentment that messages intended to persuade do precisely the opposite, sowing even more ill will.

The value of social media companies has become a controversial topic in both marketing and financial circles—as well it should. The business press is always questioning the valuations of social media companies that have gone public or have received huge rounds of venture capital funding. The equity markets can't seem to get enough of big social companies going public, whether they are profitable or not. In ten years, however, Facebook and Twitter might not even exist. The environment in which they are currently successful is predicted to undergo some extremely volatile changes in the next five to ten years.

A simple way to look at the current social media situation is to think of it as one of the first utilities of the 21st century. A hundred years ago, the landline phone, the radio, and the electric industry created great financial wealth because they brought new, life-enhancing services to the populace. Often, due to the huge cost of installation, these utilities were granted monopolistic powers in order to serve the public. They were valuable companies with predictable revenue streams providing services that united the country's citizenry. People may not have had great loyalty to the brand—in fact, many customers actively disliked the local power and phone companies— but they loved the services these utility brands brought to their homes.

As noted in the previous chapter, the emotional relationship and value that people have with the social-network brands they use is very low. Why? While people like to share their thoughts, photos, and videos with others, they are not loyal to the companies that provide this access. This duality of loving the experience but lacking loyalty to the brand—for example 20th- century phone companies—is an indicator of the predictable future for most social media companies.

As an explanation, social media is not a mature medium; it is, as we've said, in the embryonic stages of its development. New tools and apps are introduced almost daily. As this book is being written, Facebook is the biggest global social media player; its billion-plus users give Facebook the revered "network effect" for now, but Facebook will lose its absolute market dominance unless it is extremely nimble.

How nimble? Well, Facebook's Mark Zuckerberg is competing with people like Emerson Spartz, the 26-year-old president of Spartz Media, who, at the age of 12, built a site called Mugglenet that attracted 50 million page views a month from rabid Harry Potter fans. Spartz's specialty is creating viral websites—such as DailyCute, Smartphowned, Unfriendable—that appeal to high school and college students. Spartz's company creates a new website every six weeks, and 90 percent of them make triple the amount of money he invests in them. His genius is creating websites that have their own gravitational pull; they act like memes, spontaneously sparking people's interest in ways they cannot resist.

Marketers can learn much from Spartz. He is the sort of person who, in a relative instant, could easily hit upon the Next Big Thing in social media—just by riding the Zeitgeist in a different way. How might someone like Spartz exploit Facebook's vulnerabilities?

To begin with, Facebook does not have high brand loyalty with its users. Many people over 40 love Facebook, but it is rapidly losing its youngest users (who call it "MomBook"). Many digital natives simply don't use it at all, preferring instead such platforms as

Instagram, Snapchat, Pheed, AskFM, Kik, or private platforms they create themselves. Furthermore, advertising is Facebook's only revenue stream, and users are getting much less tolerant of the sort of data-mining that makes the site's targeted ads valuable to advertisers. Protecting people's private information while also exploiting it, is a difficult act to balance, and Facebook has, as yet, not perfected this requisite.

Indeed, privacy, intrusiveness, and data-protection are some of the Internet's biggest issues, in large part because companies like Facebook and Google have made them so. In an era of heightened privacy concerns, consumers might even begin to avoid companies that profit by sharing their personal data. This is already happening, in fact, as consumers seek out services and technologies that allow them to circumvent and bypass advertising. When Facebook bought the increasingly popular texting application Whatsapp for a mind-bending $19 billion in early 2014, actual users of Whatsapp were somewhat dismayed—partially, because they chose Whatsapp to avoid the reach of Facebook's marketing tentacles!

Convenience may trump privacy concerns for the majority of people, but the risk of being perceived as a privacy intruder is a very real one for marketers and service providers who do not appreciate these sensitivities. Compared to the world that is coming, however, the amount of data available to marketers today is miniscule, and the issues raised by mining are relatively simple.

While social media will continue to be a paramount part of brand marketing in the near future, behavioral data from mobile devices and other emerging technologies is the next big frontier for those who want to connect their brand with customers. The extraordinary volume and 'granularity' of data coming from mobile sources is exploding, allowing brands to interact with customers at specific locations, in real time. In the coming world of all-to-all communication, consumers will have access to what masses of people (not just their friends) are doing, and how they are interacting with retailers and brands.

In effect, consumers will become nodes in an extended neural network sending streams of information back to the cloud, giving them instant access to huge amounts of data happening in the consumer marketplace. Instead of about half of consumers sharing their experiences with the world, 100 percent of consumers' data could potentially be shared. When this sort of all-to-all communication is realized, and the technology enabling it becomes increasingly integrated into our work, lives, and even bodies—that is when the higher consciousness of the Shift Age will really begin to transform the way human beings experience life on this planet.

In this rapidly approaching new era, the connections between people will be much more robust and multi-dimensional, making today's social media platforms look laughably obsolete. On a personal level, information will not just come in the form of text and tweets, but in holographic projections, 3D models, mutual thought-pairing, and other methods enabled by technology that acts as a seamless extension of our senses. We may now type our thoughts with a keyboard, but soon we will be able to control computers with our brainwaves alone, making it possible to connect directly with someone else's brain—literally sharing their reality.

In such a world, it will be possible to solve problems much faster than we do today. Committees, meetings, and forums that take months or years to provide solutions could do the same work in a matter of minutes or hours. Faced with a global crisis, for instance, it would be possible to create an instant think tank comprised of the world's top experts, who could all communicate with each other through a universal thought translator— literally putting their minds together to solve a problem.

When we say a "new level of consciousness," this is what we mean: a world in which, through the Neurosphere, people are capable of connecting, assimilating, and creating in the realm of a universally accessible collective consciousness. As the Neurosphere expands, and the technology to access it becomes more sophisticated, people all over the world won't just connect; they will create a level of interaction and meaning of which today's technology offers only a glimpse.

Brands will be just as important in this new realm. All of those people processing information will still be looking for voices and guideposts they can trust. What will continue to change is the relationship between brands and customers. Social media gives companies the opportunity to connect directly with the consumer/customer, and to develop much deeper, more meaningful relationships with them. Increasingly, however, this communication will be a two-way exchange, and the demand for transparency will be absolute. The challenge for brand managers will be devising ways to guide people to the messages they want people to hear without appearing manipulative or disingenuous. The world in which brand managers operate will be pull rather than push, attract rather than propel, and engage rather than persuade.

Rest assured, opportunities will exist everywhere. It will just take a different kind of thinking to take full advantage of them.

CHAPTER 14

TRANSACTIVE BRANDING:
LEVERAGING COLLECTIVE CONSCIOUSNESS

The Emergence of the Neurosphere

Earlier, we discussed how people today have to manage two simultaneous realities: the physical reality, and the screen reality. We also discussed the rapidly expanding Neurosphere, and how digital natives in the Shift Age will not feel as if their lives are split in two, as many adults do today. For digital natives, physical reality and screen reality will simply be life as they know it, they will never have experienced life any other way. To them, being connected to everything in the world via screen reality will make the concept of "information overload" seem like an artifact of history—back when people worried about things like the "speed" of technological change, and the world being taken over by robots that didn't obey.

As the technologies of the Shift Age evolve, and the new generation of digital natives assimilate them into the slipstream of their daily lives, a new "collective consciousness" will evolve. One in which the planet will operate like a huge brain, and individual people will be nodes in a technologically enabled nervous system of extraordinary complexity, speed, power, and beauty.

Marketing will still occur in this world, but the existence of this ever-expanding collective consciousness will profoundly change the nature of brands and how we manage them. In the Neurosphere, brands will be able to connect with anyone, anywhere, at any time—and consumers will expect the same in return. The nature of this interaction will be different as well. The relationship between brands and consumers will be far more personal, interactive, immediate, and meaningful.

If you do it right, that is.

The idea of the Neurosphere as a whole new level of human consciousness can seem somewhat abstract and intimidating—as can anything we do not fully understand. But, it's not a complete mystery. To envision the shape the emerging Neurosphere may take, and how it might function, we can derive clues from the work done in the field of Transactive Memory, which studies the complex memory system of a group. Transactive Memory was first conceptualized 30 years ago by Daniel Wegner. Its hypothesis basically suggests the following.

"A transactive memory system is a mechanism through which groups collectively encode, store, and retrieve knowledge. Transactive memory was initially studied in couples *and* families *where individuals had close relationships but was later extended to teams, larger groups, and organizations to explain how they develop a "group mind."*

For more than 20 years, scientists have been observing and mapping the inner workings of group memory. What they have found is that the concept of "group think" might actually be more effective than individual memory. With Transactive Memory, individuals do not need to remember every single detail of a situation. They are helped by the fact that if they do not remember a particular detail, they know who, in the group, will likely have access to that information. With this kind of memory, teams use collective recall and combine different cognitive strengths to develop information and form conclusions that are not available to any one member of the team.

Transactive Memory gives us some insight into how individual humans incorporate and process the ideas, thoughts, and consciousness of other humans. In the Neurosphere, every individual will eventually have access to the combined consciousness of everyone else in the world, and will be able to synthesize that collective intelligence in an instant. This is already happening to some extent through such crowd-sourced information sites as Wikipedia and Reddit, and through certain crowd-sourced science projects that collect data from armies of volunteers all over the world. However, today's online capabilities only hint at the things that will be possible as the vastness of the Neurosphere expands.

Still, there are real-world models available to us now that can help predict the nature, form, and direction of this brave new world. Transactive Memory is not new. Long before there was a World Wide Web, or even electricity, humans formed their own small networks, closely communicating with each person in the group to form a node, which fed into a constellation of shared thoughts, out of which civilization and culture emerged. Families, clans, tribes, and corporations use Transactive Memory to store and share information about the group. Studying these interactions can give us several clues about how the Neurosphere will operate, albeit in an exponentially more complex and connected fashion.

The three key elements to developing an effective Transactive Memory system are:

- Specialization
- Coordination
- Credibility

In an effective Transactive Memory system, *specialization* means that each individual in the group must have expertise in an area other group members do not. That expertise can be proprietary information, a different perspective, a unique skill, a special talent, or any number of other distinguishing characteristics. Importantly, it should be a complementary knowledge set that the rest of the group members do not—and do not have to—recall or remember.

Coordination, in the Transactive Memory model, simply means that the individual must be able to communicate effectively with others in the network—so that, if specialized knowledge needs to be shared with the group, it can be done quickly and efficiently.

Credibility, in this context, means the extent to which other group members believe an individual's specialized knowledge is trustworthy, reliable, or accurate.

In a group or team that uses Transactive Memory effectively, these three elements work together to help make the whole of the group smarter than the sum of its parts. The same logic applies to brands. A high-quality brand evolves when a team of experts pool their talents to create a superior product or service in a specialized niche. To make that happen, the people behind the brand must be able to coordinate their activities to achieve a common goal. And, in order for the brand to be successful, consumers must believe that the brand represents a product or service they can trust.

The early elemental stages of this behavior are already developing. Many observers of the Millennial generation have seen and experienced how members of this generation, when part of a team or group, immediately collaborate by assigning tasks based upon members' expertise or passion. Millennial groups immediately "go flat" in terms of power, and rely on other members to do their part. The identity of the self functionally moves to a collective sense of self in order to accomplish the mission. Individual authority and mastery gives way to a shared, collaborative effort of the group, often resulting in much faster solutions.

As the first phase of social media is coming to a close, and cloud computing is widely utilized, people are using these technological tools of connectivity to share tasks and responsibilities. Baseball moms use Facebook to collectively manage all the coordination for their son's team, sharing responsibilities and expertise. Project teams use such tools as Google Drive and GoogleDocs to collaborate in real time to create final results fast by assigning and sharing duties and creative assignments. Mobile connectivity combined with social media allows flash mobs to materialize in one place at a certain time and then disperse.

These early-stage examples of technologically-driven Transactive Memory are clear directional signposts to what lies ahead.

In the Shift Age, the rapid development of the Internet of Things will play an important role in shaping the transactive properties of the Neurosphere. Our clothing, devices, cars, and homes are now communicating through smart technology that records everything. All of these devices and the information they share is fine-tuning the Transactive Memory capabilities of the Neurosphere, mapping human behavior through Big Data in ways that marketers will be leveraging for years and decades to come.

This Internet of Things exponentially increases the complexity of the Neurosphere, which will continue to operate more and more like a giant human brain whose abilities are amplified by the billions of smaller brains connected to it, each with a tiny portion of specialized knowledge. The method for successful brands in the Neurosphere will be to harness the positive properties of Transactive Memory to create credible nodes that cut through the noise and clutter, creating clarity and meaning amid the din of extraneous junk information that will also be an inevitable result of all-to- all communication.

The truth is, people don't want to know everything—they just want to know what they want to know, when they want to know it. So in the Neurosphere, just like in the physical world, people will gravitate toward brands with focus and purpose, and will trust brands with a proven track record—brands that can provide them with the specialized knowledge they seek. That "knowledge" can take the form of a product, service, meme, or metaphor. The important thing is that it must be useful or relevant to a life lived in multiple levels of consciousness, in a world both complicated and simplified by amazing new technologies. Even digital natives need help navigating their lives, and the brands that help them do it best are the ones that will get their attention and business.

So, how might such a brand operate in the Neurosphere?

The music service Pandora is a good example of a brand that creates its own gravitational pull. Pandora doesn't push itself on people. Rather, it attracts its audience by offering a means for people to customize their own music, effectively allowing them to create a hyper-personalized radio station—one that only plays music they like. Pandora also uses a dynamic algorithm—a form of artificial intelligence software—that identifies characteristics in the music people like, and scours its database for music with similar properties, which it adds judiciously to a customer's musical mix.

Spotify, another music service, takes the Pandora model a few steps further by allowing people to search for specific songs and albums, offering curated playlists, and giving customers suggestions for music they may like based on music they have already heard. Both Pandora and Spotify try to behave like a trusted cyber-friend—one who knows your tastes in music, and "learns" more about you the more you listen. Both services also encourage you to build a network of listeners and share musical discoveries with your friends, thereby keeping their audience engaged, extending their reach to a broader network of people, and multiplying the service's cultural influence. And, as discussed, influence in the Neurosphere is the new power.

Significantly, both Pandora and Spotify give their basic service away for free. The basic service includes advertising; what people *pay* for, in part, is the privilege of *not* having their music interrupted by "annoying" ads. Digital natives in particular have a low tolerance for intrusive advertising.

The only way they will overlook the ads is if they don't seem like advertising at all—if it is wrapped in the package of entertainment.

There is nothing futuristic about Pandora or Spotify—they are almost mainstream services at this point—but the way they adapt and interact with their customers using a form of artificial intelligence is an indication of how many other types of services will operate in the future.

Unlike wholly web-based companies like these, however, most brands must find ways of existing in both the physical and screen realities. Developing effective, complementary strategies that serve the brand in both realms is going to be an ongoing challenge for brand marketers.

Red Bull is a good, current example of a brand that knows how to market to Millenials both online and off. Red Bull is an energy drink, but it markets itself as a meme. The slogan "Red Bull gives you wings" has an almost mythological level of aspiration, implying (as it does) that Red Bull can make you fly. In the physical world, Red Bull's marketing revolves around sponsorship of sporting events— motocross races, surfing competitions, Grand Prix racing, etc.— where speed and agility are involved. More important, Red Bull has created its own sporting events— Flugtag in summer, and Crashed Ice in winter—based on the idea of flying and having a crazy, free-spirited kind of fun.

Flugtag is a competition in which teams create their own non-powered flying apparatuses and launch them over a body of water until they crash. Crashed Ice is basically downhill racing on ice skates. Both events travel around the world staging competitions in various cities, and receive a tremendous amount of free publicity in the press. The events appeal to young people as well, helping solidify Red Bull as their drink of choice for outrageous, free-spirited fun. Online, Red Bull augments these sponsorships and events with a web presence dedicated to all things fast and sporty—motosports, BMX racing, surfing, snowboarding, base jumping, auto racing, etc. It also covers video gaming and music, creating an online gathering place for anyone interested in an extremely active and adventurous lifestyle.

From a branding standpoint, the drink is superseded by its association with the lifestyle to which Red Bull drinkers aspire. In essence, Red Bull has positioned itself as a conduit for all Transactive Memory having to do with energy and adventure, and the extensions of this meme into the Neurosphere are paramount to Red Bull's success, now and in the future.

Being able to position the brand as an idea around which like-minded people can gather and commune is going to be an increasingly important skill in the Neurosphere. It will not happen simply through websites, advertising, and e-mail newsletters. It will happen as a result of leveraging the explosive power of neural networks and knowing how to transform the information available through Big Data into ideas and action.

Google knows this, which is why in 2013, it hired inventor/futurist Ray Kurzweil (author of *The Singularity is Near*), bought Boston Dynamics— one of the world's largest robotics companies—and has been snapping up robotics and artificial intelligence start-ups at an impressive clip. One particularly interesting company Google has acquired is DeepMind. It is a company that is researching something called Artificial General Intelligence (AGI), also called Strong AI, which is different from ordinary Artificial Intelligence (AI, or weak AI). It learns from its experiences and is, to some extent, self-aware. Until now, machines that think like humans have been the subject of science fiction, but DeepMind and dozens of other companies, including IBM, are on the verge of making it a reality.

Indeed, many scientific wonders first speculated in science fiction are now becoming realities. As theoretical physicist Michio Kaku reminds us in his latest book, *The Future of the Mind: The Scientific Quest to Understand, Enhance, and Empower the Mind*, it is already possible to insert a chip into the brain of someone who is completely paralyzed, connect them to a computer, and have them operate it— web surf, write emails, play video games, control a wheelchair— using only their thoughts.

At UC Berkeley, researchers can videotape people's dreams using an MRI machine that digitizes the data into an image. According to Kaku, "Computers are now powerful enough to record the electrical signals emanating from the brain and partially decode them into a familiar digital language. This makes it possible for the brain to directly interface with computers to control any object around it." It is only a matter of time before this technology will enable people to send their thoughts and emotions in an electronic "brain-mail." It is fueling research in the rapidly developing fields of Brain-Machine Interface (BMI) and Brain Computer Interface (BCI).

Two government-sponsored initiatives are accelerating this type of research. One is president Barack Obama's proposed Brain Research Through Advancing Innovative Neurotechnologies (BRAIN) initiative, and the European Union's Human Brain Project, both of which seek to map the human mind, much as the Genome Project has mapped human gene sequences. Once the human mind is mapped, unlocking the "deepest secrets of human consciousness," and it is possible to digitize human thought, Kaku theorizes that it may one day be possible to transmit human consciousness via a laser beam to the edge of the universe.

David has long foreseen this new evolutionary shift in consciousness. He launched his blog, www.evolutionshift.com, in early 2006. Later, in *The Shift Age* and then in *Entering the Shift Age*, he suggested that this new consciousness might well start to occur in the 2020s. The Neurosphere is the current technological model for this new evolutionary stage of human consciousness, which will emerge within a decade.

As he wrote in his first book, *The Shift Age*, published in 2007:

- Tools defined the Agricultural Age.
- Machines defined the Industrial Age.
- Technology defined the Information Age.
- Consciousness will define the Shift Age.

Rapid advances in the interface between humans and computers today and in the near future, suggest that these technologies will have a profound effect on the way human beings interact with one another in the next five to ten years. What is more difficult to discern is how companies can protect themselves from the inevitable disruptions such advances will cause, while simultaneously recognizing the advantages and opportunities that this new level of electronic consciousness will unveil.

Brands can become trusted nodes of this larger, connected consciousness, depending upon the trust they have earned, the value they give back to all who interface with them, and the new knowledge they develop and share. When everything is connected, much more will be known about the users of products. Appliance brands in a smart world can earn consumer trust by helping people live better, use less energy, eat healthier, exercise more effectively, etc. Sports brands such as Nike, for instance, can collect and analyze data from its users to provide valuable workout feedback to athletes on an on-going basis. The key for companies and brand managers is figuring out how to use the tools and information available to them, to deliver added value in a way that enhances the brand's relationship with the customer, thereby securing the customer's loyalty and trust. Theoretically speaking, this isn't much different from how brands have always operated. The difference is that these capabilities simply didn't exist in the past. For brand managers, then, there is intense pressure to not only understand how the Neurosphere works, but also how their brands can take maximum advantage of the opportunities that will inevitably come with it.

CHAPTER 15

MEDIATING PSYCHOLOGICAL TENSIONS OF THE SHIFT AGE

Psychological Crises and the Shift Age: Branding Opportunities for the Future

As positive and progressive as the cultural, economic, technological, and social changes ushered in by the Shift Age are likely to be, they will also generate a significant amount of psychological distress as people try to integrate an unprecedented amount of change into their daily lives. While younger sectors of the global population will assimilate these changes into their lives much more easily than people over 30, youth will be affected as well. Over the next two decades, even Millennials will begin to feel as if their kids are growing up in a world they don't quite understand.

As the Neurosphere evolves, almost everyone is bound to feel a sense of dislocation and unease as the technological ground shifts beneath their feet. History has shown us, that these kinds of cultural dissonances can create opportunities for brands to leave a lasting mark—particularly ones that help do the disrupting. Silicon Valley is full of companies that made the traditional way of doing things obsolete, and the new worlds of biotech, engineering, medicine, communications, publishing, transportation, retail, and office supplies are built on the graveyards of inventors and companies that came before them. That is the way capitalism works—by initiating cycles of creative destruction fueled by innovation.

The tectonic upheaval of the Shift Age constitutes a more profound philosophical matter for society than most people realize. The reason is that it calls into question what it means to be human, what it means to have a consciousness, and what our role and status in the universe really are. A person's sense of self—and self-worth—depends on knowing how they fit into the larger scheme of things. But if the larger scheme gets too huge and complex, and humanity's place in it is displaced by robots, computers, and various devices that can do almost anything better, faster, and more efficiently than a human being, what's left for us to do?

Many people in the working world—particularly blue-collar workers— have already felt the humiliation of being rendered obsolete by a machine. Software and computers are eliminating management and service jobs on a daily basis. Many types of jobs— mail carrier, assembly-line worker, cashier, secretary—are disappearing and will never come back. The fact is, unemployment rolls are full of people whose job skills have become obsolete in the past 20 years. In some ways, these workers are the canaries in the coalmine for the current rate of technological change. At this point, people are simply losing their jobs. Imagine what would happen if everyone began feeling more or less irrelevant compared to the automated magic around them. What if people were robbed of their purpose and meaning in life by machines that do everything for them—or worse, machines that actively compete with them? You don't have to be a futurist to see that this is a recipe for a true, humanity-wide existential crisis. There will be more than economic disruption and creative destruction in the Shift Age. Life will be dealing with the psychological alteration of humanity itself.

Past age transitions have triggered massive disruption as well, but the news hasn't been all bad. Machines eliminated jobs around the world in the 19th and 20th centuries, but subsequently created far more jobs—ones that fueled vast amounts of new wealth. Computers displaced whole job sectors in the past several decades, but then created entirely new professions and tens of millions of new jobs. Did anyone graduating college in the 1960s or 1970s see that "tech support" would be a viable profession? No—but the differences, between these past disruptive waves of change and the ones occurring in the Shift Age, are significant.

Past waves of change happened sequentially through time. One can look back at a timeline of change, of technological innovation, and see that it has been a linear, horizontal progression that accelerated through centuries, then decades. Today, in the Shift Age, the speed of change has accelerated to the point where the speed of change on this timeline is almost vertical. Innovation and disruption are constants now, occurring all the time, all around us. They are now part of our environment, the everyday reality we take for granted. There is nothing sequential about it—it is a simultaneous explosion of disruptions across all sectors that are affecting humanity in ways never seen before.

Consider the psychological issues raised by a form of artificial intelligence that is, actually, intelligent. Machines that can learn, and are programmed to teach themselves. Books and movies tend to extrapolate the arrival of intelligent machines as a doomsday scenario, but the reality is likely to be an extended period of mixed emotions and ambivalence over the expanding role of technology in our society. This isn't a mere reference to talking about the "dangers" of too much screen time for kids or the pros and cons of multi-tasking. The world is up against a once-in-a-millennia challenge to many of the inherited ideas about what it means to be a conscious human being.

Ever since *Homo sapiens* outlasted the Neanderthals more than 30,000 years ago, human beings have been the dominant intelligent life form on planet Earth. The emergence of a class of machines that will eclipse human beings in many areas will change all. As a species, the human race has never shared the earth with a rival form of intelligence. Therefore, how it will play out is yet to be determined.

The Shift Age will be the first time in human history that humans will find themselves co-habiting earth with an equal or superior intelligence. There is simply no historical guidance for this. Humanity's innate sense of species superiority—manifested in many ways when we look at our relationship to our planet and other species—will for the very first time be challenged and called into question.

Artificial Intelligence, exponentially more powerful computers, and robots that are superior and cheaper to use than humans, will all be part of a fundamental assault to our sense of self, superiority, and place in the world. In addition, when robots become more "life-like" or "human," and incorporate self-improving artificial intelligence, many of us will wonder whether the age of biological human dominance has ended.

This reality is quickly approaching. Already, people are comfortable talking to their smart phones and asking their car's navigational system for directions and restaurant recommendations. Soon, drivers may cede control of their vehicles to computers altogether. Google has spent years testing its driver-less car technology with nary an accident in hundreds of thousands of miles driven. These tests are not simply about accumulating R&D data. The larger purpose of logging millions of accident-free miles on the most congested roads in the country is to build public trust in the technology. Without this trust, the technology would not be marketable.

Virtually every major carmaker is working on its own version of a driver- less car. The current estimates range widely from a prediction that by 2035, nearly 9 percent of all cars on the road in the United States will be driver-less to bolder ones claiming 75 percent by 2040 will be driver-less. Once people start having positive experiences with this technology—crash statistics for driver-less vehicles predictably should drop markedly. The "computer" can automatically find a faster route to your destination by processing real-time traffic data. As insurance rates on driver-less cars drop—people will begin to trust these non-human mechanisms with their very lives. In time, people will begin to depend on these technologies to navigate their daily routines—not just on the roads, but also in every other aspect of their lives.

This transitional development from a human-centric world to an intelligence-centric world will be simultaneously wonderful and scary. Large portions of humanity will embrace this new way of living and will rapidly morph into acceptance of a new reality. They will favor and trust the brands that are developing transformative technologies and creating new possibilities. Brands that can lead us through this evolutionary minefield will be exalted and embraced by those in the Shift Age. They will help allay people's fears that the future contains nothing but disruption and chaos.

Since the reality of Shift Age consumers is so radically different from that of previous generations, they think differently. Market research done by Leo J. Shapiro & Associates LLC in the past few years has helped to shed some light on the psychology of Shift Age consumers. What we call the "transitional" decade between the Information Age and the Shift Age started in roughly 1995, when a huge wave of people who were kids then, are now entering the workforce. These young people did not identify with the Information Age, but they absorbed the Shift transition almost by osmosis. They are grappling with the fallout of the Great Recession, as well as the practical challenges of living in a world where expectations don't always align with reality, and where many of the rules that guided previous generations no longer apply.

What the research by Leo J. Shapiro & Associates found is that Shift Age consumers are guided by several paradoxes. Though they are the group most likely to have been affected by the Great Recession—due to large amounts of student debt and a sluggish job market—they are also the group that is most optimistic about the country's future. As a group, they are more likely to be laid off or experience disruptions in their income stream, but they are also the group that has the brightest outlook about their economic future. Psychologically speaking, the relative volatility of their economic situation does not necessarily dash their hopes and dreams. There are certainly many cynical, disaffected young people in America—and there always have been— but Shift Age consumers are used to a high degree of uncertainty and are not thrown by rapid change. Whatever happens, they are generally optimistic.

A generally positive, resilient outlook on life and the ability to rapidly assimilate technological change are two of the identifying characteristics of the Shift Age consumer. For marketers this means that, as an audience, they are receptive to ideas that will help them improve their world, and they won't have any trouble keeping up with companies that push the technological envelope. Indeed, the larger challenge for brand managers is going to be keeping up with these Shift Age generations, since their preferences and allegiances can change in an instant. Loyalty is not a given. This is a generation that likes and seeks out new experiences. Brands that want to keep up should provide the experience for them—not just in their products, but also in the whole universe of associations that the brand has with the world. Brands that sit still will stagnate quickly, and brands that have too much confidence in their historic legacy could topple easily.

There will, however, be a large percentage of humanity, including many who came of age in the 20th century, that feel threatened, lost, and disoriented. They will reactively cling to what they consider "reality" as they know it. The "Luddites" who resist an increasingly robotic world will be far more numerous and fearful than the original Luddites, who resisted the machines of the Industrial Age. The level of disruption has never been greater.

Brands have often played a significant role in helping people mediate these types of disruptions between epochs. As we saw in earlier chapters, patriotic branding in the late 19th century helped unite the U.S. into a cohesive national culture. In the early 20th century, brands helped consumers moving to cities transition from a provisional, rural way of life to an urban, cosmopolitan one. Similarly, brands can help consumers articulate and mitigate the conflict presented by the Shift Age.

Brands can provide a trusted friend that guides people from their old "reality" and helps them acclimate to the emerging new reality. This will require brands to anchor themselves to the consumer's past while it leads them into the future. This is where the nodal vision of brands in the prior chapter comes into play.

Brands will have to exist as multiple nodes mapped across the timeline of human acceptance. They will have to find ways to educate and lead those at the forefront of change—the Shift Age consumers—while at the same time providing reassurance to those who are more fearful of these huge changes. When the ground is shifting underfoot, when humanity is evolving at an exponentially faster rate, brands cannot afford to be fixed or static. Creating reliable support for consumers who are trying to retain their individual identity through this unprecedented time of change will be key.

We are with you.
We are here to help.
We understand your pain and your confusion.
We provide you with ways to better live through these unsettling times. We share what we are learning every day with you.
We help you become the new you and to understand the new reality.
We want you to help us as well, because we are all in this together.

These are the messages that the brands of the 21st century need to communicate.

CHAPTER 16

INTO THE FUTURE AND WHAT TO DO

We are now moving into the second half of the second decade of the 21st century. Ten years into the Shift Age, we live in a world where the speed of change has accelerated to the point where it is now environmental, an unavoidable yet an essential component of our daily lives. Humanity lives in the new reality of the ever-expanding Neurosphere generating, spreading, and consuming memes that course through human awareness at the speed of light. This is the first iteration of humanity that lives in a growing spatial reality, not a place-restricted reality.

This generation is the very first that will begin to share the planet with an equal or superior intelligence. The experience in a generational transfer of power, influence, and wealth unprecedented in its speed and magnitude, is about to occur. The world of accelerating technological innovation measured in months, weeks, days, and sometimes seconds—not years or decades is now. Reality no longer feels fixed but fluid, flowing in several directions at once.

As the Shift Age progresses, and the rate of change increases, disruption will be the rule, not the exception. Life will be disorienting for those locked into the legacy thinking of the past, those who are unable to adapt and co-evolve into this uncertain but exciting future will feel lost, if not abandoned.

Welcome to the most transformational time in human history. It is also the most condensed time of change in the history of brands and marketing. It's an age when both marketers and consumers will be shaken to their core by the challenges of living and working in an era that will restructure how consumers perceive themselves and their needs, and how brands communicate with the customers to fill those needs.

What do you need to do? How should you proceed as a brand marketer in these tumultuous times? How do you develop the ability to be totally fluid, adaptive, and resilient in the face of constant change, then turn around and infuse these qualities into the brand? What will a brand even mean in the years ahead?

If the above words and phrases excite you, then you can feel the energy of opportunity and creative joy needed to thrive. If the above words make you nervous or fearful, then you are no doubt wondering if you can survive in this strange new world.

The hope is that this book has made you less afraid, and has given you some tools for thinking about how to work effectively in the Shift Age, and how to take advantage of the opportunities this new age will present.

Stepping into the Future

A lot of time has been spent emphasizing how brands will be affected by disruption and change in the coming years, but brand managers can take some comfort in knowing that many of the principles that have guided brands in the past will also guide them into the future.

As discussed earlier in the book, successful brands respond to, and grow out of, the culture they are in. Whatever needs the culture has, successful brands fulfill them. Whatever fears and anxieties the culture has, responsive brands provide the necessary solace and comfort. The same will be true in the future—only the application of these principles will change.

Also, as presented in Maslow's Hierarchy of Needs—a staple for marketers for the past 60 years—there is provision for a meaningful framework to understand the psychological implications of a world in which men and their machines are co-evolving together, raising unsettling questions about the very nature of humanity.

From the perspective of Maslow's hierarchy, marketers will face three major trends in the coming years:

- **Consumers experiencing downward mobility from the forces of the Shift Age.** These are the ones being dislocated by the automation of jobs that once required higher-level human cognition, such as basic analytic and data organization/ processing functions. They will be driven by the lowest levels of branding needs: safety, esteem, and belonging.

- **People who are able to find a role in the Shift Age.** These are people who are able to hang on to jobs not easily replaced by artificial intelligence—personal service positions, or jobs that require a close reading of human emotions—but who don't directly benefit from the huge increases in productivity and output. These consumers will aspire to the need gratification of the early Shift Age: aesthetics and cognition.

- **Those who are able to embrace change.** They are equipped to take advantage of the dislocations caused by the technology of Shift Age (Neurosphere, AI, etc.). They will find abundant opportunities for gratifying lower-order needs, and will soon focus on self-actualization and, eventually, transcendence.

What follows are some high-level concepts, suggestions, dynamics, and forces that will provide fodder for those of you who are excited about this transformative time for brands. They will also be a benchmark for those of you who are nervous about whether you are capable of making the essential shifts needed to stay in the game.

Marketing Will Be Adding Value to Me

As a brand marketer, you must provide value to individuals and enhance their sense of themselves as a unique, personal brand. How can the brand you market be perceived as adding value to current and potential customers as the Shift Age unfolds?

The Flow to the Individual will continue as growth becomes increasingly capable of reaching out and connecting with the world. As people develop their own individual brands, however, they will be continuously looking for brands both large and small that can enhance their own personal brand. In many ways, then, brand identification will be stronger—and more important—than ever.

Levels 3-8 on Maslow's Hierarchy of Needs must underscore your customer relationships, particularly when it comes to addressing the individual's self-perceived needs.

Level 3: Social Needs
Level 4: Esteem Needs
Level 5: Cognitive Needs
Level 6: Aesthetic Needs
Level 7: Self-Actualization Needs
Level 8: Transcendence Needs

Some brands will succeed because they have great value to people and customers on just one of these levels. Some brands will need to address two or three of these levels of needs. Moving forward, levels 7 and 8 will become ever more important, particularly in the developed countries of the world. Connecting on these top two levels will create the deepest bonds between brand and customer during the next decade. As an individual seeks and strives for their higher aesthetic sense of self, then to self- actualization, and then finally to realize transcendence needs, she will be aiming for the highest level of association with a brand—one that involves deep trust and a high expectation of transparency. Brands that successfully connect on these levels will create deep and lasting relationships with their customers, but will have to work hard to maintain the trust on which those relationships are built.

The (BII) Brand Influence Index, introduced in Chapter 12, was developed in part to help companies measure the quality of the relationship between a brand and its customers, and to serve as a guide for companies that want to improve in that area. Brands can work their way up from Disconnected to Devoted by addressing their customers' hierarchy of needs. As the Shift Age progresses, and people's basic needs are met, brands that fulfill people's aspirations and help them achieve self-actualization will exert an ever-greater influence in the marketplace.

The Brand Influence Index will, along with Maslow's Hierarchy of Needs, become increasingly relevant over the next decade as humanity grapples with the implications of sharing the planet with a technological intelligence of growing sophistication and power. One key limitation of artificial intelligence, however, is that it doesn't have human emotions, which makes the psychological basis of the BII Index that much more important for brands that want to establish and maintain meaningful relationships with their customers.

Mazlow's Hierarchy of Needs is of course based on HUMAN needs, not the needs of a machine. Will human needs become more or less important when challenged by a non-human, but equivalent intelligence that insists on asserting its own needs? And, what happens when humans relinquish so much of their independence to technology—driver-less cars, pilot-less planes, robotic surgeons, etc.—that they become utterly dependent on it? On the other hand, what happens when robots themselves start looking and acting human? Is this good, or bad, both or neither?

These types of philosophical questions will inevitably arise as the Neurosphere expands, and our lives become more inextricably entwined with it.

Persuasion Will Be Giving and Aspirational, Not Manipulative

In the future, the trend of shifting trust from institutions to the individual will continue and may even accelerate. This could have profound implications for traditional brands that are unwilling to evolve. It will also change the dynamics of persuasion between companies and their customers.

If, for example, an institutional brand comes across as trying to manipulate consumers to buy, buy, buy—with little regard for the customer—it will be perceived as being crass, old school, and not fully trustworthy.

If, however, a brand can be perceived as generous and giving (of content, data, ideas, connections, etc.), whether an individual makes an immediate purchase or not, that generosity of spirit can serve as a foundation for a stronger, longer-term relationship that could result in multiple sales. If a brand can persuade customers that they are helping to change or improve the world, or addressing the needs of some segment of humanity, then they are positioned to attract customers with similar aspirations and values. This kind of "conscious capitalism" will become increasingly important for marketers in the coming years, especially those representing brands that want to connect with people under 30, and who like their spending to reflect their idealism.

This doesn't mean customers won't still flock to big sales. Deeply discounted prices can still drive consumers to purchase. In fact, one of the strongest post-Great Recession trends is the idea that "thrift is the new cool." Outside the luxury-brand strata, where high prices attract people, global consumers will continue to look for ways to buy at lower prices— and, in the Internet-connected world, they will be able to find them. A brand that can stand on—and honestly deliver—lower prices without a commensurate drop in quality will be able to maintain a strong relationship with its customers. The Millennial generation, in particular, is loyal to brands that deliver reliably low prices but are also perceived as giving.

Thrift stores and any "previously owned" brand marketing that can honestly align with planet-friendly views of sustainability will also appeal to new generations of customers. Such brands can even satisfy higher- level needs while delivering lower prices. If a customer's sense of self revolves around sustainability and respect for the planet, for instance, their ongoing self-actualization will include purchasing patterns that support sustainability. Such customers will seek out companies that truly embrace those values, but will shun those that are only pretending in order to ingratiate themselves to broader customer base. Sincerity and commitment are key.

Selling Will Be Sharing

If you look at how people use social media today, there is one key element that all social media platforms rely upon: people like to share. In the iterations of social media to come, sharing will continue to be a fundamental driver, albeit in different ways—especially for brands that are trying to leverage social media as a marketing tool.

The key for brands is to share with existing and potential customers in ways that do not relate solely—or directly at all—to products being offered. The "selling" is done by associating the brand with ideas and information and directional signposts that can help customers navigate their swiftly changing, information-overloaded lives. Toward that end, brands that can synthesize Big Data into understandable and usable nuggets will succeed in the next decade—because that's what customers will be looking for, especially in the area of mobile communications.

Brands Will Be Resources

The shift from brands that merely represent a product or service to brands that serve as a constellation of related resources is a direct outgrowth of the three rules above. If a brand can be perceived as a resource of reliable information beyond what they sell—as a gateway to related experiences, or a bridge to other aspirations and desires—they will command attention, frequency of interaction, and most importantly, trust.

A brand that serves as a reliable and trusted resource for advice on social or career issues will gain customers. A brand that can help bring drinkable water to the billion-plus people in the world who don't have it—their "good works" mission—will attract those whose values align with that vision. A brand that can be a resource for the etiquette of life's most difficult conversations—about parenting, divorce, death, caring for elders, managing money, etc.—can serve as a long-term resource for customers throughout their lives. Companies that connect people to information that can help them manage their everyday lives will also prove invaluable.

Companies that make products for babies and children, and food companies that provide information about cooking and meal prep, have done a relatively good job in this regard in the past. The associations are clear, and people often act on the extra information such companies provide. Going forward, brands should not fear straying farther afield from what they actually sell. In fact, such out-of-the-box excursions into other territories can connect companies with entirely new groups of consumers.

Another significant way a brand can be a resource is helping consumers navigate the unprecedented psychological and emotional disruption that will accompany the realization that people are beginning to share the planet with an equal or superior intelligence. Whether they see it as a positive or negative, people will have deep feelings about the merging of artificial intelligence, robotics, and advanced computing into their daily lives. In the world of computer-generated imagery (CGI), for instance, there is something called the "uncanny valley" effect. People like computer-generated characters, it turns out, up to the point where they are too lifelike, or almost lifelike but not quite—after which they are repulsed. The uncanny valley is the gulf of perception between something that is almost human and fully human. A machine-generated human likeness that looks too real creeps people out—because, consciously or not, they perceive the machine's human-ness as a threat to their own existence.

For this and many other reasons, there will be a great deal of tension around this coming reality. Different demographics and psychographics will experience the disruptions in a variety of ways—all of which provide opportunities for brands to offer comfort and assistance.

Cutting-edge early adapters, trans-humanists, and technologists will embrace this evolutionary development and will respond favorably to brands that lead and shape new ways to think about sharing the planet with another form of intelligence. Many more people will feel deeply threatened, at risk, and unsettled about this development. These modern- day Luddites will respond positively, however, to a brand that honors humanity above technology and values human intelligence over artificial quasi-intelligence.

Managing brands amid this fluid chaos will be an enormous challenge, but also an invigorating one. How does one position the brand relative to the disruptive reality that millions of people are feeling? If people are feeling overwhelmed—economically, psychologically, emotionally—and cast aside by rapid technological change, is there an opportunity? Is it possible for a brand to become a resource to both those who are embracing transformation and those struggling to make the shift?

In the coming years, every single brand will need to decide how to navigate this new reality. These are not small questions, and there are no easy answers, but they must be asked—and answered—if brands are to evolve.

Marketing in the Big Data Era

Brands and those that market them need to fully understand how much the reality of Big Data is going to profoundly change marketing. Big Data is ushering people into the world of real-time anthropology and sociology. Having now entered a time of where, when and what people do, the assimilated likes can be immediately known to others. Make no mistake; this is one of the greatest transformational changes in the history of brands and marketing.

At the highest level, there are four major things that all marketers must embrace in the Big Data Era.

1. The ability to know more about your customers than has ever been possible, and to communicate with them in a highly personalized manner.

2. The need to create a higher level of sharing around data, in ways that deepen trust and increase the perception of transparency.

3. The ability to communicate with your customers wherever they are, and predict where they might be going and what they might soon be doing.

4. The ability to utilize unlimited data to understand and calibrate marketing almost literally moment by moment.

Let's look at each of these new opportunities:

1. *The ability to know more about your customers than has ever been possible, and to communicate with them in a highly personalized manner.*

Today, people live in an environment that records most everything done. This ever-smarter world keeps tabs on the majority of every aspect of the consumers' lives, particularly if they are technologically connected. At the meta level, this pervasive connectedness will provide marketers with unparalleled granular data about each consumer, making it possible to message them with increasing specificity.

Market research no longer has to translate the difference between what consumers say they want, and what they really want. Big Data is live, real-time market research on a massive scale.

In a world where convenience can often trump almost everything, including privacy, there is great value in making it easier for the consumer to say yes. Humans are flattered when it becomes clear that someone has taken the time to learn more about them. "Make it about me, and make it easy for me," is certainly a smart seller/buyer concept. Perhaps the best example today is Amazon and their Prime membership. As a Prime customer, one can buy what one wants easily and with no shipping cost. They have a long record of the consumer's previous purchases, so they know a great deal about them. Using that knowledge, they alert the user to other products for which they might have an interest, and they do it in the context of an established relationship. The consumer is, therefore, more likely to trust their recommendations.

2. The need to create a higher level of sharing around data, in ways that deepen trust and increase the perception of transparency.

When social media is used, the member knows that the sharing, likes, and follows say a lot about them, and that this information is then used to customize ads targeted to their interests. In the post-Snowden era, people are more conscious of "Big Brother" watching, and are more careful about what they share and with whom they share it—but they still share. The new era of Big Data will erode privacy even more, though, as our entire lives are tracked and recorded. Consequently, consumers will think hard about where to place their trust, particularly if it involves sharing sensitive personal data.

Big Data means that data will be flowing into brands from people, chips, bots, GPS, algorithms, appliances, infrastructure, and satellites. Almost everywhere, everything will be transmitting everyone's data. Brands that want to use this massive data stream to market to customers will be able to do much more than simply target consumers with ever more specific ads. Brands can use this vast treasure trove of information to develop and package messaging that helps people navigate their lives and make important decisions—and even create customized experiences. Large data sets, graphically displayed, about things of interest to the customer and their demo/psycho-graphic, will also be well-received as an added value from the brand. Sharing in the era of Big Data is not one-way, it is every way—which means it will open up all sorts of creative possibilities for interaction with customers.

3. The ability to communicate with your customers wherever they are, and predict where they might be going, and what they might soon be doing.

By the end of 2016, the majority of global cell-phone users will have smart phones that provide a multitude of data and offer a variety of ways to message consumers. Of course, the first level is simple location in a general sense. The developing next level is specific locations inside stores. A cereal maker will soon be able to know when a potential customer is actually walking down the cereal aisle in the supermarket. Armed with this information, marketers can target the right person, at the right time, in the right place, with the right price—a level of specificity unprecedented in the history of marketing.

In addition, humans are fairly predictable. If a marketer knows where a person was, and what they did last week, they can predict with a fair degree of accuracy what that person might do this week. This is anticipatory marketing with a high probability of transactions.

4. *The ability to utilize unlimited data to understand and calibrate marketing almost literally moment by moment.*

The Internet of Things is now providing massive amounts of personal data about how we live and what we like. It is accumulating data about what is happening at this moment in a rapidly increasing number of locations. Soon, data about almost any aspect of society, human activity and behavior will be available, providing a real-time profile of the world in action at any given moment. Marketers will have more information at their fingertips, more quickly, than ever before. The real issue will be how to extract useful and valuable information from the zettabytes of data being generated. Marketing companies and brands will have to employ chief data officers and people who can convert all this information into understandable, actionable intelligence. Data is just information, but curated data is knowledge, and knowledge is, of course, power.

Brands Will Be Nodes of the Larger Human Network/Consciousness

Humanity is getting ever more connected. The Internet as the web is the metaphor for the early 21st century; nodes, synaptic networks, and the holographic processing of the human brain will be the metaphor for the rest of the century. The Neurosphere is a synaptic and pulsating entity that will serve as the technological model for a new form of consciousness. This neuro-consciousness will continue to evolve over the next two decades, and it is where much of the future of brands will reside.

This Neurosphere can be viewed as a global network of nodes. Every person, every company, every brand will be a node of this network. Marketers must now think of their brands as nodes of this net. They can no longer think of their brand as simply products or services to be distributed to the consumer, but as nodes that can push and pull to the global market in its entirety.

This is where transactive branding—based upon the discussion of Transactive Memory in Chapter 14—comes into play. What role can a brand's node or nodes play in the collective consciousness of cyberspace, of Digispace? What can the brand promise to be and do in this new realm? In the collective space of the Neurosphere, how will a brand's nodes serve the collective greater good?

These questions go beyond for what a brand and its products stand, and into the realm of what a brand represents for all of connected humanity. Creating nodes with a higher purpose, or the promise of trusted advice, or the ability to connect like-minded people—these are the sorts of activities in which marketers will be increasingly involved.

Big brands may have multiple nodes serving different constituencies. Different sub-brands and different geographical markets may be different nodes. A multi-national corporation may have multiple nodes in different languages and nations, as well as multiple product nodes. Given that all can be accessed from anywhere, there will have to be a consistency of messaging, sharing, and mission across the entire nodal landscape—which is no small task.

Small companies may only have a single node in the Neurosphere. If so, that node must be clear and trusted; a singular node that encapsulates the entire image, values, and being of the company.

In all cases, these nodes will be real-time, interactive, resource-and information-rich vortexes that will be constantly morphing due to the synaptic interactions they have with the rest of the Neurosphere.

Information travels much faster through networks than it does up and down hierarchies. Silos can no longer exist. Speed of dissemination and reaction become critical. A node must be a dynamic, bright place of sharing, not a dark, non-responsive hole of indifference.

Meme Marketing

As discussed in Chapter 10, memes are ideas and thoughts that course through human awareness and consciousness with viral speed as people like, share, post, tweet, and re-tweet them around the globe.

In the ever-accelerating electronic connectedness of the Shift Age, marketing will be increasingly meme-like. Indeed, brand marketers are already trying to create memes for their brands. Like shooting stars, these memes shine brightly for a short time, then die—which is the nature of memes. Memes are spontaneous and difficult to manufacture, but when they work, they work wonderfully.

One value of a meme is that those who help make it go viral tend to be somewhat invested in it. When sharing a brand meme, people are tacitly saying they support the brand, even if only in some limited way.

Another value of a meme is its immediacy and breadth. It moves fast across a wide audience, creating a sense of newness and topicality. This isn't the "New! Improved!" false newness of traditional marketing. Rather, effective memes speak to something current that a brand thinks should be shared. Some memes connect to ideas bubbling up in the zeitgeist, such as 99/1 or the need for alternative energy, and many are humorous or entertaining. Brands that want to avoid controversy should go the entertaining route. Brands that truly stand for something—that represent some idea that appeals to people on various levels—can hit several of Maslow's needs at once.

The fact that Millennials embrace the Shift Age power of influence more than their elders means that this generation will both create memes and support them. The decades-old conundrum of how to reach younger demographics can be addressed with generational memes—because one that resonates in the right way can reach an entire generation at once.

While there will continue to be structured thinking about brand campaigns in the future, there will also be more creative, inspired, immediate creation of memes. These memes can of course support the larger brand campaign. In success mode, memes will be a part of any brand campaign. What is meme-like within a given campaign is the question brand marketers must now consider.

Space Versus Place

Humanity lives in a world where there is no time, distance, or place limiting human communication. The Concept of Place as a restrictive, limiting geographical area is dying. The 21st century is the first century in which humanity begins to live in the spatial reality of the networked world. Increasingly, the thought is of global citizens connected by the global Neurosphere.

Even strictly local businesses such as restaurants, theaters, and museums can enlarge their customer base by dispensing with place limitations in their marketing. Create a fun, lively node for your local place-based establishment and you will likely find that the node has attracted global citizens. How this happens is sometimes a bit of a mystery, but it does happen—and it happens because there is no geography in the Neurosphere.

The Evolving New Level of Consciousness

Humanity is moving toward an evolutionary shift in consciousness that will begin to occur in the next two decades. The global stage of human evolution is here, and more connected than ever. As we become more connected in the Neurosphere, space will supplant place in the evolving sense of self.

Breakthroughs in neuroscience are happening all the time, rapidly increasing the knowledge about how the brain works. The brain can now be connected to technology in ways that allow it to be controlled by the user's thoughts. Brain/computer interface technologies are becoming cheaper and more sophisticated. The screen reality and the Neurosphere seem to be synaptically replicating the brain, opening a new technologically-driven consciousness.

The Internet of Things is creating a connected, Big Data-driven, technologically-based machine consciousness. When this develops in conjunction with Artificial Intelligence, robots, and super-computing, there will be a globally connected new technological consciousness that will, in part, be self-aware. The big question is: Will this accelerate a counter-balancing human shift in consciousness as well?

Digital Natives, the first full generation of the 21st century, will develop a profoundly different consciousness as they mature into adults. While their individual world will be a hyper-personalized, customized experience, their sense of self—developed as much online as off—will be more shared and less individualized. Instantly shared information will make it possible for them to act collectively, when necessary. That power, combined with their numbers, will allow them to wield a great deal of influence. This new, collective consciousness, flowing from the Neurosphere, will be one of the most transformative developments of the next two decades.

This new evolutionary shift represents a step toward transcendence. Remember what Maslow's 8th hierarchical level was? Transcendence.

Admittedly, it is very hard to imagine this evolutionary shift into a higher level of consciousness. What will it feel like? How will it change communications? How will it alter humanity's view of itself?

The technologies discussed in this book are moving towards this new reality, and the profound differences in generations are pointing the way. The three forces of the Shift Age—The Flow to Global, The Flow to the Individual, and Accelerating Electronic Connectedness—are creating the space and time for this consciousness to begin.

By following the suggestions in this chapter, regarding how to market brands, you will be taking clear, sound, practical steps towards being able to navigate this emerging consciousness as it unfolds. Think of this book as preparation for the journey. There will be bumps and obstacles along the way, but brands and marketers that are prepared for the disruptions to come are much more likely to emerge intact, healthy, and successfully transformed, ready to meet other challenges that the future will inevitably bring.

Shift. Brand Shift. Now is the time it starts. Take action.

References

Introduction

Gerzema, John, and Lebar, Edward Lebar. *The Brand Bubble: The Looming Crisis in Brand Value and How to Avoid It*. San Francisco: Joseey-Bass, 2008. Print.

Houle, David. *The Shift Age*. Chicago: Sourcebooks, 2011 (orig. 2007). Print. Electronic.

Houle, David. *Entering the Shift Age: The End of the Information Age and the New Era of Transformation*. Naperville: Sourcebooks, Inc., 2013. Print. Electronic.

The Brand Influence Index. Chicago: Leo J. Shapiro & Associates LLC, 2012. Print.

Chapter 1

Aronczyk, Melissa, and Powers, Devon. *Blowing up the Brand: Critical Perspectives on Promotional Culture*. New York: Peter Lang Academic Publishers, 2010. Print.

Clifton, Rita, Ahmad, Sameena, Allen, Tony, Anholt, Simon, Barwise, Patrick, Blackett, Tom, Bowker, Deborah, Chajet, Jonathan, Doane, Deborah, Ellwood, Iain, Feldwick, Paul, Frampton, Jez, Gibbons, Giles, Hobsbawm, Andy, Lindemann, Jan, Poulter, Allan, Raison, Maxwell, Simmons, John, and Smith, Shaun.
Brands and Branding. London: Profile Books Ltd, 2009. Print.

Gerzema, John, and Lebar, Edward Lebar. *The Brand Bubble: The Looming Crisis in Brand Value and How to Avoid It*. San Francisco: Joseey-Bass, 2008. Print.

Leo J. Shapiro & Associates, LLC. *The National Poll*. Chicago: Leo J. Shapiro & Associates, LLC, 2010. Print.

Leo J. Shapiro & Associates LLC. *Study of Trends and Attitudes among CMOs*. Chicago: Leo J. Shapiro & Associates LLC, 2010. Print.

Markoff, John. *Computer Wins on 'Jeopardy!': Trivial, It's Not*. Science: The New York Times, 2011. Web. <http://www.nytimes.com/2011/02/17/science/17jeopardy-watson.html?_r=1&pagewanted=1&hp

Ries, Al, and Ries, Laura. *The Origin of Brands: Discover the Natural Laws of Product Innovation and Business Survival*. New York: HarperCollins, 2004. Print.

The Fournaise Marketing Group Report: 2011 Global Marketing Effectiveness Program. Web. <https://www.fournaisegroup.com/ceos-do-not-trust-marketers/>.

Chapter 2

"100 YEARS: From "See the USA in your Chevrolet" to "Like a Rock," Chevy ads run deep." Automotive News. 31 October 2011. Web. <http://www.autonews.com/article/20111031/CHEVY100/310319942/100-years:-from-see-the-usa-in-your-chevrolet-to-like-a-rock-chevy>.

Baughman, James L. "Television Comes to America, 1947-57." Wisconsin: University of Wisconsin, 1993. Web. <http://www.lib.niu.edu/1993/ihy930341.html>.

Bevan, Andrew, and Wengrow, D. *Cultures of Commodity Branding*. Walnut Creek: Left Coast, 2010. Print.

Chernow, Ron. *Titan: The Life of John D. Rockefeller, Sr.* New
    York: Random House, 1998. Print

"Sep 7, 1813: United States nicknamed Uncle Sam." This Day in
    History. History.com. 24 May 2014. Web.
    <http://www.history.com/this-day-in-history/united-states-
    nicknamed-uncle-sam>.

Holmes, Richard. *The Age of Wonder: How the Romantic
    Generation Discovered the Beauty and Terror of Science.*
    New York: Pantheon, 2008. Print.

Holt, Douglas B. *How Brands Become Icons: The Principles of
    Cultural Branding.* Boston: Harvard Business School, 2004.
    Print.

Houle, David. *The Shift Age.* Chicago: Sourcebooks, 2011 (orig.
    2007). Print. Electronic.

Houle, David. *Entering the Shift Age: The End of the Information
    Age and the New Era of Transformation.* Naperville:
    Sourcebooks, Inc., 2013. Print. Electronic.

Johnson, Bradley. *From 'See the USA in your Chevrolet' to 'Like a
    Rock,' Chevy Ads Run Deep.* Advertising Age. 2011. Web.
    <http://adage.com/article/special-report-chevy-100/100-years-
    chevrolet-advertising-a-timeline/230636/#1950>.

Leo J. Shapiro & Associates LLC. *Study of Trends and Attitudes
    among CMOs.* Chicago: Leo J. Shapiro & Associates LLC,
    2010. Print.

Moor, Liz (Ed.). *The Rise of Brands.* Oxford: Berg Publishers, 2007.
    Print.

Rivkin, Steve, and Sutherland, Fraser. *The Making of a Name: The inside Story of the Brands We Buy*. Oxford: Oxford UP, 2004. Print.

McLeod, Saul. *"Maslow's Hierarchy of Needs."* Simple Psychology, 23 May 2014. Web. <http://www.simplypsychology.org/maslow.html>.

Vintage Chevrolet Online. Vintage Chevrolet Archives. 'Dinah Shore Sings "See the USA in Your Chevrolet."' 23 May 2014. Web. <http://www.vintagechevrolet.org/articles/VCO_2001019_dina hsh ore.htm>.

Chapter 3

"About Amazon." Amazon. 16 June 2014. Web. <http://www.amazon.com/Careers-Homepage/b?ie=UTF8& node=239364011>.

Houle, David. *The Shift Age*. Chicago: Sourcebooks, 2011 (orig. 2007). Print. Electronic.

Houle, David. *Entering the Shift Age: The End of the Information Age and the New Era of Transformation*. Naperville: Sourcebooks, Inc., 2013. Print. Electronic.

Kurzeweil, R. "The law of accelerating returns." Kurzweil Accelerating Returns. Web. <http://www.kurzweilai.net/the-law-of-accelerating-returns>.

"Cable News Network." Encyclopaedia Britannica. 16 June 2014. Web. <http://www.britannica.com/EBchecked/topic/87632/Cable-News-Network-CNN>.

"MTV." Forbes. 16 June 2014. Web. <http://www.forbes.com/companies/mtv>.

Chapter 4

Brooks, David. "The Romantic Advantage." New York Times: New York, 2013. Print. Web. <http://www.nytimes.com/2013/05/31/opinion/brooks-the-romantic-advantage.html?_r=0>.

Car and Driver. May 2010 Issue. Web. 16 June 2014. Web. <http://www.caranddriver.com/features/2013-tata-nano>.

Houle, David. *The Shift Age.* Chicago: Sourcebooks, 2011 (orig. 2007). Print. Electronic.

Houle, David. *Entering the Shift Age: The End of the Information Age and the New Era of Transformation.* Naperville: Sourcebooks, Inc., 2013. Print. Electronic.

Interbrand. "Sort." *Brand Equity by Geographic Region,* 2013. 22 May 2014.

Leo J. Shapiro & Associates LLC. *The Brand Influence Index.* Chicago: Leo J. Shapiro & Associates LLC, 2012. Print.

Chapter 5

Houle, David. *The Shift Age.* Chicago: Sourcebooks, 2011 (orig. 2007). Print. Electronic.

Houle, David. *The Shift Age.* NAW 2012 Executive Summit. 2012. Web. <http://www.naw.org/files/events/es12_Houle_---_The_Shift_Age.pdf>

Houle, David. *Entering the Shift Age: The End of the Information Age and the New Era of Transformation.* Naperville: Sourcebooks, Inc., 2013. Print. Electronic.

Chapter 8

Houle, David. *Entering the Shift Age: The End of the Information Age and the New Era of Transformation*. Naperville: Sourcebooks, Inc., 2013. Print. Electronic.

Chapter 9

De Chardin, Pierre Teilhard. *Le Phenomene Humain*. Paris: Editions du Seuil, 1955. *The Phenomenon of Man*. London: Wm. Collins Sons & Co., Ltd, 1959. *The Phenomenon of Man*. New York: Harper & Row, 1959. *The Phenomenon of Man*. New York: HarperCollins Publisher, Inc. 1975, 2002. Print. Web. <http://www.amazon.com/The-Phenomenon-Pierre-Teilhard-Chardin/dp/0061632651#reader_0061632651>.

Chapter 10

Dawkins, Richard. *The Selfish Gene*. New York: Oxford University Press, 1976. Print.

Houle, David. *The Shift Age*. Chicago: Sourcebooks, 2011 (orig. 2007). Print. Electronic.

Houle, David. *Entering the Shift Age: The End of the Information Age and the New Era of Transformation*. Naperville: Sourcebooks, Inc., 2013. Print. Electronic.

Chapter 11

Houle, David. *Entering the Shift Age: The End of the Information Age and the New Era of Transformation*. Naperville: Sourcebooks, Inc., 2013. Print. Electronic.

Chapter 12

Leo J. Shapiro & Associates LLC. *The Brand Influence Index.* Chicago: Leo J. Shapiro & Associates LLC, 2012. Print.

Chapter 13

Fottrell, Quentin. Yelp deems 20% of user reviews 'suspicious.' A study of flagged write-ups shows how some try to game the system. Market Watch. The Wall Street Journal. 2013. Web. <http://www.marketwatch.com/story/20-of-yelp-reviews-are-fake- 2013-09-24>.

Leo J. Shapiro & Associates LLC. *Social Media Buzz Helps Sink Tropicana Squeeze.*

Luca, Michael, and Zervas, Georgios. "Fake It Till You Make It: Reputation, Competition, and Yelp Review Fraud." Boston: Harvard Business School, 2013. Web. <http://www.hbs.edu/faculty/Pages/item.aspx?num=45151>.

Chapter 14

The Fournaise Marketing Group Report: 2011 Global Marketing Effectiveness Program. Web. <https://www.fournaisegroup.com/marketers-lack-credibility>.

Houle, David. Evolution Shift. 2006. Blog-Web. <www.evolutionshift.com>.

Houle, David. *Entering the Shift Age: The End of the Information Age and the New Era of Transformation.* Naperville: Sourcebooks, Inc., 2013. Print. Electronic.

Houle, David. *The Shift Age.* Chicago: Sourcebooks, 2011 (orig. 2007). Print. Electronic.

Kaku, Michio. *The Future of the Mind: The Scientific Quest to Understand, Enhance, and Empower the Mind.* New York: Doubleday, 2014. Print.

Leo J. Shapiro & Associates LLC. "The Shift Age Consumer." Chicago: Leo J. Shapiro & Associates LLC, 2010. Print.

Wegner, D.M. Transactive memory: A contemporary analysis of the group mind. In B. Mullen & G.R. Goethals (Eds.), Theories of group behavior (pp. 185-208). New York: Spring-Verlag, 1986. Web. <http://www.wjh.harvard.edu/~wegner/tm.htm>.

Chapter 15

Leo J. Shapiro & Associates LLC. "The Shift Age Consumer." Chicago: Leo J. Shapiro & Associates LLC, 2010. Print.

"Top 5 Predictions About The Future Of Driverless Cars." Aol Autos, 2012. Web. <http://autos.aol.com/article/top-5-predictions-about-the-future-of-driverless-cars/>

Worstall, Tim. "9% Of Cars To Be Driverless Cars By 2035." Forbes, 2014. Web. <http://www.forbes.com/sites/timworstall/2014/01/01/9-of-cars-to-be-driverless-cars-by-2035/>

Biographies

David Houle

David Houle is a futurist, strategist, and speaker. Houle spent more than 20 years in media and entertainment. He worked at NBC, CBS, and was part of the senior executive team that created and launched MTV, Nickelodeon, VH1, and CNN Headline News.

Houle has won a number of awards. He won two Emmys, the prestigious George Foster Peabody award, and the Heartland award for "Hank Aaron: Chasing the Dream." He was also nominated for an Academy Award. He is the Futurist in Residence at the Ringling College of Art + Design.

He has delivered some 600 speeches on six continents and twelve countries. He is often called "the CEOs' Futurist" having spoken to or advised 2,500+ CEOs and business owners in the past seven years.

This is his sixth book.

Owen Shapiro

Owen Shapiro has always been fascinated with how people 'make up their minds' which has lead him to pursue a diverse range of research and discovery projects both in academics and in business.

Owen is a market researcher, strategist, and speaker. Owen spent more than 30 years in customer insights and market strategy. He has a careerlong interest in helping launch innovative start-up companies—several which have become well-known brands—including: Staples, PetSmart, Sports Authority, Ulta, and Five Below—and some that are just starting their journeys.

Owen is a guest presenter at the University of Chicago, where he received his MA and MBA—drawing on his combination of real-world experience with clients, his training in social science theory, and his grounding in research methods.

CPSIA information can be obtained at www.ICGtesting.com
Printed in the USA
LVOW01s2344181214

419433LV00003B/4/P

9 780990 563501